Words for Students of English

Vocabulary Series Editors
Holly Deemer Rogerson
Lionel Menasche

Volume 5

WORDS
for Students of English

A Vocabulary Series for ESL

Holly Deemer Rogerson
Carol Jasnow
Suzanne T. Hershelman

Pitt Series in English as a Second Language

Ann Arbor
University of Michigan Press

First published by the University of Michigan Press 1992
Copyright © 1989, University of Pittsburgh Press and
    the English Language Institute, University of Pittsburgh
All rights reserved
ISBN 0-472-08215-9
Published in the United States of America by
The University of Michigan Press
Manufactured in the United States of America
♾ Printed on acid-free paper

2004   2003   2002   2001   12   11   10   9

Illustrations by Suzanne T. Hershelman

Contents

Foreword

The objective of this series of vocabulary texts for the student of English as a foreign language is to facilitate the learning of approximately 3,000 new base words. Vocabulary learning has long been deemphasized in language teaching, much to the detriment of the students, who have mostly been left to fend for themselves. We thoroughly agree with Muriel Saville-Troike, who states, "Vocabulary knowledge in English is the most important aspect of oral English proficiency for academic achievement" (*TESOL Quarterly*, vol. 18, no. 2, p. 216).

With the present lack of comprehensive vocabulary texts suitable for both classroom use and home study, this series is intended to support teachers in preparing effective vocabulary lessons so that they can meet their students' urgent need for an increased lexicon. We present here a selection of base vocabulary items and some of their derived forms (i.e., the noun, verb, adverb, and adjective of the same stem) together with a series of exercises designed to help students remember the new words and use them in context.

This text has been used in an experimental edition in the English Language Institute, and modifications suggested by its use have been incorporated in the present version.

Christina Bratt Paulston
Director, English Language Institute
University of Pittsburgh

Acknowledgments

A series such as this depends greatly on the cooperation and hard work of numerous people:

Christina Bratt Paulston and Holly Deemer Rogerson originated the idea for the series.

Christina Bratt Paulston provided ongoing support for the series.

Mary Newton Bruder, Carol Jasnow, Christina Bratt Paulston, and Holly Deemer Rogerson developed the first version of the list of approximately 600 words assumed known.

Holly Deemer Rogerson developed the original pool of words from which the 150 topic word lists were chosen. She also organized the word lists and, with Lionel Menasche, provided general management of the project, including authors' drafts, revisions, editing, illustrations, duplicating, testing, and typing.

Ideas for word lists, format, and exercise types were contributed by Betsy Davis, Gary Esarey, Suzanne T. Hershelman, Carol Jasnow, Carol Moltz, Lionel Menasche, Holly Deemer Rogerson, Dorolyn Smith, and Linda M. Schmandt.

Lionel Menasche and Holly Deemer Rogerson were responsible for final revisions of content with input from classroom testing by Isabel Dillener, Jeanette Courson, Caroline Haessly, Pat Furey, Carol Jasnow, Ken Rose, Linda M. Schmandt, Jill Sherman, Tom Swinscoe, and Lois Wilson.

Courtenay Meade Snellings and Dexter Kimball provided valuable editorial assistance in content revision and proofreading.

JoEllen Walker and Anna Mae Townsend typed several drafts of the manuscript.

Lisa Krizmanich assisted during the testing phase.

Introduction

Volumes 1–7 of *Words for Students of English* present English base words,* with definitions, examples, and exercises. The texts may be used as core texts for vocabulary learning classes or as supplementary texts in reading, speaking, and writing classes. They may also be used for individual study.

Each unit focuses on one topic so that the words being presented can be practiced in meaningful contexts. Some of the new words in each unit are directly related to the topic, while others are less directly connected. Most of the words in a given unit can be used in a variety of contexts.

Volume 1 assumes a knowledge of 600 base words in English. Starting from this point, new words are presented in each unit, with the definitions, examples, and exercises in Volumes 1–6 *containing only vocabulary which has been previously learned.* There are 25 units in each of Volumes 1–6, while Volume 7 has 22 units. The first units in Volume 1 contain only about ten base words each in order to allow the students to become familiar with the format of the units. After the first units, each unit in Volume 1 contains approximately fifteen base words. In Volume 2, there are approximately fifteen base words in each unit. In Volumes 3 and 4, each unit contains fifteen to twenty base words; in Volumes 5 and 6, there are approximately 25 base words per unit; and in Volume 7, there are approximately 32 base words in each unit. On completion of the series of seven volumes, students will have learned approximately 3,700 base words.

Given that Volume 1 assumes a knowledge of 600 base words, the level of Volumes 1 and 2 can be loosely described as beginning, Volumes 3 and 4 as intermediate, Volumes 5 and 6 as high intermediate or advanced, and Volume 7 as advanced.

Selection of Words and Unit Topics

The 600 assumed words upon which Volumes 1–6 are based were chosen by a panel of experienced ESL teachers at the University of Pittsburgh as the group of words which are most typically learned by ESL students during their first two years of middle

---

*"Base" may be defined variously in lexical analysis, but for our present pedagogical purpose it implies any alternant from which other forms are derived. It is frequently impossible to say which form of a word is the most basic.

school or high school ESL classes. The words presented in Volumes 1–7 were selected according to usefulness from a variety of word-frequency lists. The authors and editors added other words to the topics at suitable levels of difficulty. In volumes 5 and 6 special attention is given to two- and three-word verbs.

In many cases students have to learn words with more than one meaning or with meanings that may vary according to context. A decision was made in each such instance as to whether the meaning in the new context was different enough to warrant further definition or similar enough for the students to extrapolate from what they had previously learned. These decisions were based on dictionary definitions and authors' or editors' personal judgments. For example, a word such as *beat* might appear in these contexts: (a) beat the opposing football team, (b) beat a drum, (c) a beat of a heart, (d) beat a person. Contexts (b) and (d) (meaning = strike) were judged close enough to allow extrapolation of meaning from one context to another, but (a) and (c) were thought to require separate definitions.

We have assumed that when a student learns a new vocabulary item, an approximate meaning for the word is assimilated, and that meaning is linked to the context in which the word was first encountered. Then, as the student meets the word in other contexts, the initially learned, approximate meaning is expanded and refined. Hence, many words are not only used several times in the unit in which they first appear, but are also used in later units.

The unit topics were chosen and ordered according to their perceived relevance to the students' lives, that is, their communicative usefulness. Most topics are covered in one unit in each volume, but certain broad topics, for example "School," are repeated twice within the same volume, in which case they are marked (A) or (B). A few topics, such as "Religion" and "Banking," due to the difficulty or abstractness of the words associated with them, are not covered in the first volume. Certain other topics whose words were perceived as tangible and easy, for example, "Telephone" and "Post Office," are completed in the first two volumes.

It should be noted that the repetition of each topic, at times within the same volume and always in at least one subsequent volume, allows for review and recycling of the material learned. Thus, long-term retention of the vocabulary is facilitated.

Format and Suggestions for Teachers: Volumes 1–6
(Note: Volume 7 has a different format, described in the introduction to that volume.)

Flexibility in using this vocabulary series has been a prime consideration in planning the format and exercises of the units. Therefore, although suggestions are given in the following paragraphs, it is assumed that teachers in different situations will decide according to their own students' needs whether work should be done in or out of class, orally or in writing, and with or without direct assistance from the teacher. The pace at which classes can proceed through each volume will vary greatly, depending on the students' motivation, study habits, and general workload, as well as the degree of emphasis the teacher wishes to place on productive vocabulary skills.

Each unit in Volumes 1–6 has the same format. The five sections of each unit are as follows.

WORD FORM CHART   STUDY EXERCISES
DEFINITIONS AND EXAMPLES   FOLLOW-UP
INTRODUCTORY EXERCISES

The WORD FORM CHART presents base words and some or all of their related forms, categorized by part of speech. In Volumes 1 and 2, an effort was made to simplify the charts by omitting many derived or related forms which were either not common, or not useful for students at this level, or not easily recognizable from a knowledge of the base form. After Volume 2, more related forms are added because the students can handle more as they progress in learning the language. Decisions on what forms to omit were made by authors and editors on the basis of experience gained during testing of these materials with linguistically heterogeneous classes. Teachers in different educational contexts should consider supplementing the charts according to their own students' needs and their ability to absorb more material. For example, many words could be added by giving antonyms formed from words already given (planned/unplanned, honest/dishonest).

In the NOUNS column of the charts in Volumes 1 and 2 only, nouns which normally or frequently refer to humans are marked by the symbol ⚲. When a noun, as defined in the unit, can be either human or nonhuman, the symbol is in parentheses: (⚲). Gerunds are not included in the charts. Nouns have not been marked "count" and "non-count" because so many nouns function in both ways.

In the VERBS column, irregular past tenses and past participles are in parentheses following the verbs. In cases where more than one past tense or past participle is acceptable, the more regular one is included in the chart. Thus, for example, in the Volume 1, Unit #4 Word Form Chart no irregular forms are listed for *forecast* because the regular form *forecasted* is also currently acceptable.

In the ADJECTIVES column, we have included any present or past participles that appear prenominally as adjectives, as well as any regular adjectives. We have not included in this column nouns which form Noun-Noun modification patterns.

The next section, DEFINITIONS AND EXAMPLES, gives the meanings of the words as well as example sentences which are usually related to the topic of the unit. The form chosen for definition is not always the base form. Other forms are sometimes chosen for greater ease of definition or learning. In all definitions and examples, only previously learned words are used. This applies also within the set of definitions in each unit. Thus, the words in each set of definitions are presented in an order which allows their definition and exemplification using only previously introduced words.

Grammatical information is given in the definitions by means of the following conventions: "to" is used before a verb to indicate the verb form, articles are used with nouns whenever possible to indicate that the word is a noun, and parentheses enclose prepositions that may follow a verb. Words with more than one meaning are cross-referenced to definitions in earlier units when new definitions are given. Extra information (e.g., irregular plurals and abbreviations) is given within braces ({ }). Separable two- or three-word verbs are labeled while inseparable ones are left unmarked.

This section, together with the Word Form Chart, can be efficiently handled as work assigned for intensive individual study, followed by discussion in class of questions raised by students. At this point the teacher may also wish to elaborate on certain definitions and give further examples.

Writing explicit definitions of words using the intentionally limited vocabulary available results in some rather broad definitions and others that are limited to certain aspects of the meaning. The deliberate compromise here between precision and generality is designed to make the text fully accessible to students by avoiding the major weakness of many other vocabulary texts: defining new items with words that are themselves unknown to the learner. The easily understood broad definitions, which may take the form of a standard verbal definition, a picture, or a list of examples, are then refined by further exposure to appropriate examples in this unit and series and in the students' later reading. Also, students can usefully refer to a bilingual dictionary in conjunction with studying the example sentences given.

After the Definitions and Examples section, there is a three-tiered system of exercises sequenced to take the student from easy, open-book, fairly controlled exercises through more difficult, less controlled exercises to a final phase with communicative exercises.

The first part of the sequence consists of INTRODUCTORY EXERCISES. These are designed to acquaint the students with the new words in the unit and lead them to an initial understanding of the words by using the Definitions and Examples section. We recommend that these brief and easy exercises be done with books open, orally or in writing, immediately after the teacher's first presentation of the new words.

The next section in each unit, headed STUDY EXERCISES, is a longer and more difficult set of exercises designed to be used by the students for individual study or for oral or written work in class. In Volumes 5 and 6, this section includes an analogies exercise similar in format to that of the Graduate Record Examination (GRE).

The final section is the FOLLOW-UP. This includes a dictation and more open-ended communicative exercises designed to be done after the students have studied the words. The latter may be done orally in class, or teachers may request written answers to selected questions.

Each volume also contains an INDEX listing all the base words presented in that volume. Words in the preceding volumes and the assumed words are given in separate appendices in Volume 1–5. With each word is listed the volume and unit where it is presented. In Volume 6, there is both an index for the volume and an appendix combining all the words in the assumed list and in Volumes 1–6.

An ANSWER KEY at the end of each volume provides answers for all the exercises in the Study Exercises sections, except where a variety of answers is acceptable. Answers are not provided for the Introductory Exercises or the exercises in the Follow-Up so that the teacher can choose to use these exercises for homework or testing purposes if desired.

Production and Recognition

Although a distinction between vocabulary known for recognition and that known for production is often propounded, the actual situation is probably best represented by a continuum stretching from mere recognition to production which is accurate both semantically and syntactically. The exercises in Volumes 1–6 cover the full range of this continuum so that teachers wishing to stress productive vocabulary knowledge will have ample opportunity to give their students feedback on the use of the new words in their speech and writing. However, the goal of many teachers will be to increase their students' recognition vocabularies as rapidly as possible, with the expectation that those words which students meet again frequently in other contexts and have a use for will gradually become part of their productive vocabularies. Teachers with this goal of recognition vocabulary development in mind will wish to proceed more rapidly through the units and deemphasize those exercises requiring productive capabilities, for example, by limiting their corrections to semantic errors, rather than correcting syntactic mistakes as well.

In Volume 7 the new words in each unit are classified into two groups: words for production and words for recognition. The rationale for the different format of Volume 7 is given in the introduction to that volume.

Words for Students of English

Government (A)

Word Form Chart

NOUN	VERB	ADJECTIVE	ADVERB
abolition	abolish	abolished	
advocate	advocate	advocated	
approach	approach	approaching	
communism		communist	
communist			
conservative	conserve	conservative	conservatively
dignity	dignify	dignified	
distribution	distribute		
		drastic	drastically
drop	drop		
liberal	liberalize	liberal	liberally
liberality			
mayor			
measure			
reform	reform	reformed	
reformation			
reformers			
refusal	refuse	refused	
regulation	regulate	regulating	
		regulated	
deregulation	deregulate	deregulated	
right			
	run against		
	run for		
socialism		socialist	
socialist			
state			
	step aside		

NOUN	VERB	ADJECTIVE	ADVERB
sympathy	sympathize	sympathetic	sympathetically
sympathizer			
takeover	take over		
visa			

Definitions and Examples

1. **mayor** [the head of a city government]

   We elect a **mayor** every four years in this city.
   The **mayor** is the top person in our town government.

2. **visa** [an official document which permits a person to enter a foreign country]

   Americans do not need a **visa** to visit Canada, but they need one to enter Japan.
   She went to the French embassy to apply for a **visa** for her trip to Paris.

3. **sympathize** [to understand and share a person's feelings or ideas, especially when he or she has a problem]

   We **sympathized** with him when he lost his job.
   I do not have any **sympathy** for that political party; I do not like their ideas about the environment.
   I usually discuss my problems with my older brother; he is more **sympathetic** than my father.

4. **run for** [to compete for a political position]

   He is **running for** mayor in the next election.

   A: How many people are **running for** president?
   B: One from each of the four major parties.

5. **run against** [to compete against someone in an election]

   Jimmy Carter **ran against** Ronald Reagan in the 1980 U.S. presidential election.
   She **ran against** four opponents and won.

6. **refuse** [to insist on not doing something]

   The child **refused** to eat the vegetables.
   The current mayor has **refused** to run again, so his party must find another candidate.

7. **distribute** [to give to a variety of people]

   The teacher **distributed** the test papers to the students.
   Before the election, the government **distributes** information about where to vote.

8. **abolish** [to cancel a law or system]

   Most of the citizens want income tax **abolished**.
   The government is considering **abolishing** the compulsory education law.

9. **regulate** [to restrict or limit by laws]

   Most governments carefully **regulate** immigration.
   The school has **regulations** against students smoking.

10. **communism** [a political and economic system in which property is not privately owned and is available to all as needed]

    In a **communist** society, the farmers do not own their own land.
    The **Communist** party in the United States does not have much power because it does not have many members.

11. **socialism** [a political system in which production and distribution are in the hands of the people or the government]

    Communists feel that **socialism** is an imperfect form of communism.
    Moscow is the capital of the Union of Soviet **Socialist** Republics (the Soviet Union).

12. **advocate** [to think something is good and publicly support it]

    The Communists **advocate** the abolition of private ownership of land.
    People running for president often **advocate** lowering taxes.

13. **state** (a) [a nation or a division of a nation]

    The United **States** consists of 50 **states**.
    Under a Communist or Socialist government, most or all land belongs to the **state**.
    Socialists believe that the economy should be **state** controlled.

    (b) [3-2: condition]

    His business is in a terrible **state**; he is losing thousands of dollars a week.

14. **right** (a) [a power given by law or tradition]

    In a democracy, the citizens have the **right** to vote for their political leaders.
    Americans consider their **right** to free speech to be very important.

    (b) [assumed: the opposite of left]

    She made a quick turn to the **right**.

    (c) [assumed: correct]

    His answer to the question was **right**.

15. **conservative** [opposed to major changes; wanting to maintain existing conditions and views; traditional]

> His opinions are very **conservative**; he does not want the situation to change very much.
> The **Conservatives** are a major political party in England.
> Some societies are more **conservative** than others.

16. **liberal** (a) [believing in progress and change]

> The **liberal** parties are advocating greatly increased government spending on education.
> He is a **liberal** who strongly supports strengthening the labor unions.

(b) [generous]

> That company is very **liberal** with its salaries.

17. **dignity** [the characteristic of worthy and honorable behavior]

> He handled the problem with **dignity**. He did not raise his voice or show his displeasure.
> People expect judges and people in high political positions to be **dignified** in their actions.

18. **approach** (a) [to go toward something or someone]

> The day of the election is **approaching**.
> The politician **approached** the group of people and began to talk to them.

(b) [a way of looking at an issue or problem]

> The liberal **approach** to social problems is usually quite different from the conservative one.
> Many people disagree with the government's **approach** to the country's economic problems.

19. **measure** (a) [an action taken by a government or group concerning some issue]

> The government has announced new **measures** to protect the citizens from crime.
> They will have to take **measures** to avoid an increase in the rate of inflation. One possible **measure** would be to establish price controls.

> (b) [2-5: to find the size or amount of a thing]

> > She **measured** the length and width of the table.

20. **drastic** [extreme; sudden]

> Many people felt that the measures taken by the government were too **drastic**.
> Stable governments try not to make **drastic** social changes.

21. **drop** (a) [to let something fall]

    He **dropped** his books on the floor by accident.

    (b) [to fall or decrease]

    The temperature **dropped** drastically during the storm.

22. **reform** [to make a large political or social change; to improve]

    While he was running for president, he promised to **reform** the tax laws.
    Many people are demanding educational **reforms**.

23. **step aside** [to permit someone else to take your place]

    The candidate promised to **step aside** as the leader of his party if he did
      not win the election.
    Many people feel that it is time for the older leaders to **step aside**.

24. **take over** {separable} [to take control of something]

    The winner of the election will **take over** the position at the beginning of
      next month.
    The prisoners attempted to **take over** the prison, but the guards quickly
      regained control. It was the second time in a month that they had tried
      to **take** it **over**.

Introductory Exercises

A. Match each word with its definition.

_____ **1.** to compete against someone in an election

_____ **2.** to restrict or limit by law

_____ **3.** the head of a city government

_____ **4.** to take control of something

_____ **5.** a way of looking at an issue

_____ **6.** to let something fall

_____ **7.** extreme; sudden

_____ **8.** to insist on not doing something

_____ **9.** to cancel a system

_____ **10.** to compete for a political position

_____ **11.** an official document which permits a person to enter a foreign country

_____ **12.** to give to a variety of people

_____ **13.** to think something is good and publicly support it

_____ **14.** a power given by law

_____ **15.** opposed to major changes

_____ **16.** a nation or a division of a nation

_____ **17.** believing in progress and change

_____ **18.** to permit someone else to take your place

a. abolish
b. advocate
c. approach
d. communism
e. conservative
f. dignity
g. distribute
h. drastic
i. drop
j. liberal
k. mayor
l. measure
m. reform
n. refuse
o. regulate
p. right
q. run against
r. run for
s. socialist
t. state
u. step aside
v. sympathize
w. take over
x. visa

B. Answer each question with a word from the word form chart.

1. What can you do if you do not want to do something?
2. What do you feel for your friend when a member of his family dies?
3. What do you usually need in order to enter a foreign country?
4. Who is the top person in a city or town government?
5. What should the government do to a system that is bad?
6. What do we call a person who is against change?
7. What is another word meaning "law" or "rule"?
8. What is a major improvement made by a government?
9. What should a person do if he can no longer do his job satisfactorily?
10. What does a newly elected government do after an election?
11. Name two political systems.
12. What do politicians do to actions which they like?
13. What does the Red Cross do with food during a disaster?
14. What characteristic should a public official have?

Study Exercises

C. Write **T** if the sentence is true and **F** if it is false.

_____ 1. Conservative people like drastic changes.

_____ 2. If you have a right to do something, the law permits you to do it.

_____ 3. In a Socialist system the state makes many political and economic decisions.

_____ 4. The government should abolish good things.

_____ 5. Communism supports the owning of property by individuals.

_____ 6. Small children are usually dignified.

_____ 7. To solve a problem, first you need a good approach to the problem.

_____ 8. In a democracy candidates run for office against each other.

_____ 9. A friend does not need your sympathy if something bad has just happened to him.

_____ 10. Socialism is more similar to communism than democracy is.

_____ 11. Some countries are divided into states.

_____ 12. People usually refuse to do things that they love to do.

_____ 13. The government should reform systems that work well.

_____ 14. When you advocate something, you do not tell anyone else about it.

D. Complete the analogies with a word or phrase from the word form chart.

1. president : nation :: _____ : city

2. ticket : plane :: _____ : country

3. change : law :: _____ : system

4. celebrate : birth :: _____ : death

5. apply : school :: _____ : political position

6. quit : job :: _____ : political position

E. Read the passage and answer the true or false questions that follow.

     In comparison to the political situations in Europe and Latin America, politics in the United States is often considered to be quite boring. While in any American election there are usually at least two candidates running against each other, a common
5 complaint is that the candidates' positions on the issues are often very similar.
     The American system is basically a two-party one, with the two major parties being the Democrats and the Republicans. In addition, many other smaller parties exist, including the Socialist
10 party and the Communist party. However, the approaches to

political and economic issues which are advocated by many of
these smaller parties are not viewed sympathetically by the
majority of the voters. Thus, most American voters typically
choose between the Republican and Democratic candidates who
15   are running for each position.

     But what is the choice between a Democratic candidate and a
Republican one? In theory, Republicans are more conservative
than Democrats, who tend to be comparatively liberal. However,
within both parties, there are both conservative and liberal groups.
20   The result is that the position of a liberal Republican concerning a
certain issue may be exactly the same as that of a conservative
Democrat.

     Although this type of politics can be called boring, it does
provide stability for the American government. When a new
25   president takes over and reforms are begun, they tend to involve
gradual changes and not drastic ones. And although one candidate
may suggest quite different measures to attack a problem, he or
she will rarely refuse to cooperate with whoever wins the election
once that person takes over.

1. How many candidates run against each other in a typical United States

     election? _____

_____

2. Why are many of the smaller parties not well supported in the United

     States? _____

_____

3. Which of the two major parties is more conservative? _____

_____

4. How do changes normally occur after elections in the United States? Why?

_____

_____

Follow-up

F.   Dictation: Write the sentences that your teacher reads aloud.

     1. _____

     2. _____

     3. _____

     4. _____

     5. _____

G. Answer the following questions.

    1. Who is the mayor of your city or town?

    2. Name some rights that citizens in your country have. Do women have the same rights as men?

    3. Is your country divided into states? How many?

    4. Can you visit any other countries without a visa? Which ones?

    5. Does your country have more than one political party? If so, which ones are more liberal? More conservative?

    6. Name some things regulated by the national and local governments in your country.

    7. Describe an important problem faced by your country. What measures is the government taking to solve this problem?

    8. Has your country had any major reforms in the last ten years? Explain.

    9. Does your country have a Communist party? A Socialist party? What percentage of the citizens sympathize with each of these parties?

   10. Name something that you would abolish if you had the chance.

H. Explain the system of political parties in your country. What does each party advocate?

UNIT

2

Health (A)

Word Form Chart

NOUN	VERB	ADJECTIVE	ADVERB
	affect	affected	
anticipation	anticipate	anticipated	
		apparent	apparently
	bear	bearable	bearably
		unbearable	unbearably
	bring on		
cessation	cease	ceaseless	ceaselessly
		unceasing	unceasingly
cheer	cheer up	cheery	cheerily
	come down with		
condition		conditional	conditionally
		unconditional	unconditionally
confidence		confident	confidently
	confide in	confidential	confidentially
depression	depress	depressed	depressingly
		depressing	
drug	drug	drugged	
effect	effect	effective	effectively
		ineffective	ineffectively
	feel up to		
healer	heal	healed	
		healing	
injection	inject	injected	
			lately
mood		moody	moodily
		oral	orally
shape	shape	shaped	
shoulder	shoulder		
symptom		symptomatic	

12

NOUN	VERB	ADJECTIVE	ADVERB
temperature			
throat			
treatment	treat	treatable	
		treated	
wound	wound	wounded	

Definitions and Examples

1. **cease** [to stop] síːs

   The pain **ceased** soon after he had taken the pills.
   The doctors worked **ceaselessly** to find a cure for the disease.

2. **throat** [the front of the neck and the part of the body inside the neck that takes in food and air]

   She had a cold, and her **throat** hurt.
   He could not breathe because a piece of food was
       stuck in his **throat**.

3. **shoulder** (a) [the part of the body from the neck to the top of the arm]

   He hurt his **shoulder** in the football game.
   He carried the heavy box on his **shoulder**.

   (b) [to take responsibility]

   When her mother became ill, she **shouldered** the job of taking care of her
       little brothers and sisters.
   Who will **shoulder** the cost of producing more power?

4. **symptom** [a sign or mark on or in the body which shows that a person is sick]

   A high fever is a serious **symptom**.
   The first **symptom** of his illness was a pain in his throat.

5. **wound** [an injury or a cut]

   A doctor should see that **wound** immediately.
   He was **wounded** during the battle.

6. **mood** [the way you feel emotionally]

   I am always in a better **mood** when the sun is shining.
   Some medicines can drastically alter a person's **mood**.

7. **drug** [a medicine; a chemical substance that has an effect on the body]

   The doctor is using several **drugs** because my symptoms are so varied.
   The sale and use of many mood-altering **drugs** is illegal in the United
       States, but many people use them.

8. **effect** [the result of an action]

   The drug had no **effect** on the patient's symptoms; her illness continued.
   The instructor wanted to **effect** a change in my exercise habits.

   Patient: Does this drug have any side **effects**?
   Doctor: Yes. It may make you feel sleepy.

9. **affect** [to have an effect on]

   The new drug **affected** some patients but not others.
   After the heavy rains, there was a lot of flooding; everyone was moved
      out of the **affected** areas.

10. **depression** [a long-lasting bad or sad mood]

    The patient has been in a deep **depression** since he learned that his
       disease may kill him.
    She always drinks too much alcohol when she feels **depressed**.

11. **treat** [to use something to improve or change someone's or something's
    condition]

    Doctors sometimes **treat** their patients' depression with drugs.

    A: What **treatment** did the doctor recommend?
    B: Only rest in bed.

12. **orally** [by the mouth]

    You should take this medicine **orally** four times a day.
    An **oral** language is often quite different from its written form.

13. **temperature** (a) [a fever]

    She has had a high **temperature** for several days and feels quite weak.
    If your child has a **temperature**, you should keep him or her home from
       school.

    (b) [how hot or cold something is]

    The **temperature** of the water was warmer than the **temperature** of
       the air.

14. **heal** [to get better or make better, especially a wound]

    The wound should **heal** within two weeks if there is no infection.
    The cut **healed** completely, without leaving a mark.
    That doctor has **healed** many people who had bad injuries.

15. **confident** [certain; having trust in one's own or another's capabilities]

    The doctors are **confident** that she will totally recover.
    People should have **confidence** in their doctors.

16. **confidence** [trust that information will be kept secret]

>   The doctor told me, in **confidence**, that he is planning to leave that hospital soon.
>   I was given **confidential** information about Jane's symptoms.

17. **cheer up** {separable} [to make someone's mood improve]

>   We visited her in the hospital in order to **cheer** her **up**.
>   It is very difficult to **cheer up** a depressed person without actual medical treatment.

18. **come down with** [to become sick with]

>   She **came down with** a serious disease and died two days later.
>   I always **come down with** a cold at least twice each winter.

19. **bring on** [to cause]

>   Too much exercise **brought on** the old man's heart attack.
>   Many people think that being cold and wet will **bring on** a cold.

20. **feel up to** [to feel well enough to/for]

>   My wound is almost healed, but I do not **feel up to** playing tennis yet.
>   He has not **felt up to** working since his illness began.
>
>   A: Do you **feel up to** eating some soup?
>   B: No, thanks. I'll just have tea.

21. **condition** (a) [a previous requirement for another action to occur]

>   The doctor is permitting him to leave the hospital on the **condition** that he stay in bed and rest at home.
>   Her employment is **conditional** upon her finishing college within one year.
>
>   > (b) [2–6: state]
>   >
>   > When the patient's **condition** got worse, the doctor put him in the hospital.

22. **lately** [recently]

>   She has been feeling better **lately**; for the past two weeks she has been able to get out of bed each day.
>   The cost of living has gone up a lot **lately**.

23. **anticipate** [to expect]

>   We are **anticipating** that she will be able to leave the hospital soon.
>   The doctors do not **anticipate** that he will live much longer.
>   The children waited for the holiday with great **anticipation**.

24. **injection** [medicine given under the skin with a needle]

Most children do not like to get **injections**.
The nurse **injected** some pain medicine into his arm.
Some drugs must be **injected** because they cannot be taken orally.

25. **apparent** [obvious; clear] 明らかな

It is **apparent** that the patient's condition is serious; he is having difficulty breathing.
Apparently the drugs are working—her condition is improving steadily.

26. **shape** (a) [condition; state]

He is not in good **shape**; running only a short distance makes his chest hurt.
To be "in **shape**" means to be in good **shape**.

(b) [a form]

I baked a cake in the **shape** of the letter T.
The child drew several **shapes** on her paper.

27. **bear (up) (under)** [to live with a condition although it is painful or unpleasant]

She **bore (up under)** the pain of her illness well and rarely needed to take drugs for it.
The pain in his tooth was **unbearable**, so he rushed to the dentist.
The doctor said that she could not give me any more medicine now and that I would have to **bear up** for a few hours longer.
He could not **bear (up under)** his responsibilities and finally killed himself.

Some Additional Words: Names of Illnesses

cholera	mumps
flu (influenza)	pneumonia
malaria	tetanus
measles	typhoid

Introductory Exercises

A. Match each word or phrase with its definition.

____	**1.** a sign or mark on the body which shows that a person is sick	**a.** anticipate
____	**2.** to stop	**b.** apparent
____	**3.** the result of an action	**c.** bear up under
____	**4.** a long-lasting bad mood	**d.** bring on
____	**5.** an injury or cut	**e.** cease
____	**6.** by the mouth	**f.** cheer up
____	**7.** to make someone's mood improve	**g.** come down with
____	**8.** a fever	**h.** condition
____	**9.** to make or get better	**i.** confident
____	**10.** to fall sick with	**j.** depression
____	**11.** to expect	**k.** drug
____	**12.** recently	**l.** effect
____	**13.** to cause	**m.** feel up to
____	**14.** a previous requirement for an action to occur	**n.** heal
____	**15.** medicine given with a needle	**o.** injection
____	**16.** to live with a condition although it is painful or unpleasant	**p.** lately
____	**17.** condition	**q.** mood
____	**18.** obvious; clear	**r.** orally
____	**19.** to feel well enough to/for	**s.** shape
____	**20.** to use something to improve or change someone's or something's condition	**t.** shoulder
____	**21.** certain	**u.** symptom
____	**22.** the way you feel	**v.** affect
____	**23.** to have an effect on	**w.** temperature
		x. throat
		y. treat
		z. wound

B. Answer each question with a word or phrase from the word form chart.

1. Name two parts of your body.
2. Name two ways to give someone medicine.
3. Name two moods.
4. What do you hope a drug will be?
5. What should you do to a wound?
6. What do you hope that a wound will do quickly?

7. What is a symptom of many illnesses? *temperature*
8. What do patients hope their pain will do?
9. What do you hope your doctor has?
10. When did something happen if it didn't happen long ago?

Study Exercises

C.   Write **T** if the sentence is true and **F** if it is false.

____   **1.** We often use the word <u>if</u> when we state a condition.

____   **2.** Your shoulder is part of your leg.

____   **3.** People who are unbearably depressed sometimes commit suicide.

____   **4.** An effective treatment for a wound will cause healing.

____   **5.** If you feel up to something, you definitely should not do it.

____   **6.** When someone tells you something in confidence, you should keep it a secret.

____   **7.** When a wound heals, it becomes worse.

____   **8.** The anticipation of going into the hospital depresses some people.

____   **9.** If you come down with an illness, you are affected by that illness.

____   **10.** If you are depressed, you need to be cheered up.

____   **11.** A person who is in shape can run a kilometer easily.

____   **12.** If you have a wounded foot, you may have difficulty walking.

____   **13.** People want their doctors to be confident.

____   **14.** Drugs are used only for medical treatment.

D.   Fill in the appropriate preposition.

While George Jones was running (1) _____ the office of president, he suddenly came (2) _____ (3) _____ a serious illness. The illness was probably brought (4) _____ by the stress of running (5) _____ so many competitors. After a few days in the hospital, he realized that he was not going to feel (6) _____ (7) _____ continuing his fight for the election, and he decided to step (8) _____ . Another member of his party, John Smith, agreed to take (9) _____ for him. Jones's family was cheered (10) _____ by his decision to quit the race because they had been afraid all along that he would not be able to bear (11) _____ (12) _____ the stress of the election.

E. Write the word or phrase from the word form chart which is the antonym of each of the following.

1. to heal _____

2. to cheer up _____

3. to begin _____

4. long ago _____

5. effective _____

6. depressed _____

7. surprising _____

8. bearable _____

F. Complete the analogies with a word or phrase from the word form chart.

1. sunny : weather :: cheery : _____

2. solve : problem :: heal : _____

3. clue : crime :: _____ : illness

4. nearby : space :: _____ : time

5. visa : document :: _____ : symptom

6. helpful : advice :: _____ : drug

G. In each blank, write the most appropriate word or phrase from the word form chart.

Although people usually look for medical treatment to aid their recoveries from illnesses and wounds, some research has shown that a patient's (1) _____ may play a very important part in his recovery. Those people who (2) _____ a medical procedure with fear do not seem to respond as well to their medical treatment as patients who feel (3) _____ about the procedure and their own futures. Therefore, a(n) (4) _____ attitude in some way must help a person to (5) _____ the stress of experiencing medical problems. Doctors often do not wish to (6) _____ a patient whose mood is too (7) _____ . The doctors feel that their physical treatments will not be (8) _____ and prefer to wait for their patient to (9) _____ before beginning any medical procedure. Doctors are aware that there is more to healing than pills and (10) _____ .

Follow-up

H. Dictation: Write the sentences that your teacher reads aloud.

1. _____

2. _____

3. _____

4. _____

5. _____

I. Answer the following questions.

1. What kind of mood are you in today? Why?
2. Name some common illnesses. What are the typical symptoms of each?
3. Have you had any injections lately? Why?
4. What is the best treatment to follow when you have a temperature?
5. How do you cheer yourself up when you feel depressed?
6. How do you know when you are coming down with a cold?
7. What do you feel confident about? Why?
8. How you bear up under painful treatment at the dentist?
9. What are you anticipating in the next few weeks?
10. What kinds of drugs do you take orally?
11. How do strong drugs affect people when they are not taken for medical reasons?

J. Complete the story.

Mary is depressed because she has a lot of work to do, and she is coming down with a cold. . . .

Weather/Geography

Word Form Chart

NOUN	VERB	ADJECTIVE	ADVERB
	blow over		
channel	channel		
	clear up		
current			
gloom		gloomy	gloomily
horizon		horizontal	horizontally
indication	indicate	indicative	
		indicated	
indicator			
latitude		latitudinal	latitudinally
	let up		
longitude		longitudinal	longitudinally
		lousy	lousily
moisture	moisten	moist	moistly
optimum		optimum	
		optimal	optimally
phenomenon		phenomenal	phenomenally
swamp	swamp	swampy	
	turn into		
uneasiness		uneasy	uneasily
unit		unitary	
unity			
vapor	vaporize	vaporous	
		vast	vastly
vegetation	vegetate	vegetative	
	wash off		
wood(s)		wooded	

Definitions and Examples

1. **let up** [to become less severe; to stop]

   > If the storm does not **let up** soon, we will not be able to continue on this road.
   > The rain **let up** only twenty minutes after it had begun.

2. **moist** [damp; a little wet]

   > It rained a few hours ago, and the ground is still **moist**.
   > You must **moisten** the stamp to make it stick to the envelope.
   > The sun gradually dried the **moisture** on the street.

3. **indicate** [to show]

   > The moisture on the grass **indicates** that it rained here lately.
   > The clear sky to the west is an **indication** that it may be sunny here soon.

4. **gloomy** (a) [depressingly dark]

   > The weather has been **gloomy** today; the sun has not shone all day.

   (b) [depressed; sad]

   > I was in a bad mood yesterday and felt really **gloomy**.

   (c) [with no hope]

   > His view of the future is quite **gloomy**; he predicts another world war soon.

5. **clear up** (a) [to become clear]

   > I hope this gloomy weather **clears up** soon.

   (b) {separable} [to make clear]

   > The police will **clear up** the mystery if they can find some clues.
   > They want to **clear** it **up** by the end of this week.

6. **swamp** (a) [an area of wet land partly or totally covered with water]

   > Some dangerous animals live in that **swamp**.
   > It is difficult to cross the **swamp** because the land is so soft.

   (b) [to flood with water or as if with water]

   > I am so **swamped** with work that I do not have time to sleep.

7. **lousy** {informal} [very bad]

   > The weather has been **lousy** all week. I wish the sun would shine.
   > His grades are so **lousy** that no college will admit him.

8. **vegetation** [the total plant life in an area]

   The area is covered with **vegetation**. The weather there must be damp.
   There is very little **vegetation** in the desert.

9. **wood(s)** {usually plural} (a) [a small forest]

   Our farm is surrounded by **woods**.
   The little children were frightened when they got lost in the **woods**.

   (b) [2-3: the substance from trees used for making furniture, houses, etc.]

   That chair is made of **wood**, not metal.

10. **vast** [very large]

    There are **vast** swamps in South America where no people can live.
    A **vast** number of soldiers were killed in World War II.

11. **blow over** [to go away without causing any problems]

    The storm we had been afraid of **blew over** and did not cause any damage.
    The argument that I have been having with my parents has finally **blown over**.

12. **current** (a) [the forward movement of water in a river or ocean]

    You should not try to swim in this area; the **current** is too dangerous.
    A warm **current** flows off the coast of the northeastern United States.

    (b) [2-17: existing now]

    A: What is the **current** dollar-yen exchange rate?
    B: I don't know. I didn't see the news today.

13. **channel** (a) [a narrow sea between two pieces of land]

    The English **Channel** lies between England and Europe.

    (b) [the deeper part of a river]

    The larger ships must stay in the **channel** or they will hit the bottom.

    (c) [a source of television communication]

    My old TV set receives only two **channels** clearly.
    There are six TV **channels** in that city.

14. **horizon** [the place in the distance where land and sky seem to meet]

    We could see a ship on the **horizon**.
    They could not see the **horizon** because of the tall buildings.

15. **horizontal** [level with the horizon]

    Her dress had **horizontal** lines on it.

16. **latitude**

> Tokyo lies at about the same **latitude** as Washington, D.C.; the two cities have similar climates.

17. **longitude**

> In order to specify the location of a point on the earth's surface, you must give its latitude and **longitude**.

18. **optimum** [most favorable for some purpose]

> I think that the **optimum** temperature for swimming is 90° F.
> Many people think that the **optimum** number of children is two.

19. **phenomenon** {plural: phenomena} [a fact or event that can be seen]

> There are some dangerous weather **phenomena** in the mountains; for example, there are sudden and severe storms.
> Scientists try to explain **phenomena** with physical laws.

20. **uneasy** [a little worried; uncomfortable]

> Being in the swamp makes me **uneasy**. I am afraid of getting lost.
> Speaking in front of a group makes Bill very **uneasy**.

21. **turn into** (a) [to become]

> Water **turns into** ice below zero degrees Celsius.

    (b) {separable} [to make something become another thing]

> In the past, people tried to **turn** various metals **into** gold.

22. **wash off** {separable} [to wash the surface of something]

> The car is dusty. We should **wash** it **off**.
> We have to **wash off** these toys.

23. **unit** [a specific quantity used as a standard of measurement]

> The inch is the smallest **unit** of distance measurement in the English measurement system.
> The **units** of temperature measurement in the Fahrenheit and the Celsius systems are quite different.

24. **vapor** [a substance in its gaseous state]

> When there is a lot of water **vapor** in the air, the day is humid.
> If you heat a liquid until it is hot enough, it will turn into its **vaporous** state.

Introductory Exercises

A. Match each word or phrase with its definition.

_____ 1. damp; a little wet

_____ 2. very bad

_____ 3. with no hope

_____ 4. a small forest

_____ 5. very large

_____ 6. to become clear

_____ 7. the movement of water in a river or ocean

_____ 8. to show

_____ 9. to go away without causing any problems

_____ 10. to become less severe; to stop

_____ 11. the total plant life in an area

_____ 12. an area of wet land partially or totally covered with water

_____ 13. a narrow sea between two pieces of land

_____ 14. to wash the surface of something

_____ 15. the place in the distance where land and sky seem to meet

_____ 16. to become

_____ 17. a substance in its gaseous state

_____ 18. a little worried; uncomfortable

_____ 19. a specific quantity used as a standard of measurement

a. blow over
b. channel
c. clear up
d. current
e. gloomy
f. horizon
g. indicate
h. latitude
i. let up
j. longitude
k. lousy
l. moist
m. optimum
n. phenomenon
o. swamp
p. turn into
q. uneasy
r. unit
s. vapor
t. vast
u. vegetation
v. wash off
w. wood

B. Answer each question with a word from the word form chart.

1. What two measurements are required to specify a geographical location?
2. What is a small forest?
3. What may be dangerous in a river?
4. What do we hope storms will do? (three answers)
5. What is the opposite of "tiny"?
6. How can you describe a dark, rainy day?
7. How may you feel when you are alone in the street at night?
8. What is a very wet area of land?
9. What is the deep part of a river?
10. What should you do to your car if it is dirty?

11. What are used to state measurements?
12. What do you see in the distance when you are on a ship in the ocean?
13. What do you call something which is perfect for its purpose?
14. What is another word for "gas"?

Study Exercises

C. Write **T** if the sentence is true and **F** if it is false.

_____ 1. Sunlight is not a phenomenon.

_____ 2. Trees and plants are examples of vegetation.

_____ 3. A swamp is similar to a desert.

_____ 4. Dark clouds are an indication of an approaching storm.

_____ 5. Forests are unusually smaller than woods.

_____ 6. If the storm lets up, the weather will be worse.

_____ 7. An ounce is a unit of weight measurement.

_____ 8. There are vast deserts in the Middle East.

_____ 9. Boiling water produces vapor.

_____ 10. "Uneasy" means "difficult."

_____ 11. Television sets have channel selectors.

_____ 12. A storm is not an example of lousy weather.

_____ 13. It is usually gloomy at noon on a sunny day.

_____ 14. The equator is a line of longitude.

_____ 15. Moist areas usually have more vegetation than dry areas.

D. Match each two- or three-word verb with its synonym. You may use a letter more than once.

_____ **1.** run against

_____ **2.** bear up under

_____ **3.** blow over

_____ **4.** run for

_____ **5.** bring on

_____ **6.** clear up

_____ **7.** step aside

_____ **8.** cheer up

_____ **9.** let up

_____ **10.** take over

_____ **11.** come down with

_____ **12.** wash off

_____ **13.** feel up to

_____ **14.** turn into

a. to go away without damage
b. to get better
c. to make someone's mood better
d. to become less severe
e. to clean the surface
f. to survive
g. to cause
h. to become sick with
i. to become
j. to compete with
k. to moisten
l. to indicate
m. to gain control
n. to feel well enough to
o. to compete for
p. to permit someone to take your place

E. Complete the analogies with a word or phrase from the word form chart.

1. night : day :: desert : _____

2. illness : get better :: storm : _____

3. solid : liquid :: liquid : _____

4. stormy : weather :: _____ : mood

5. symptom : illness :: _____ : problem

6. small : tiny :: big : _____

7. nicest : house :: _____ : condition

8. car : bus :: _____ : forest

9. injured : wounded :: _____ : worried

F. In each blank, write the most appropriate word from the word form chart.

The swamps which exist in various parts of the world have certain characteristics in common. The thick (1) _____ which grows in a swamp tends to hide the sun and give a(n) (2) _____ appearance to the area. The air is quite (3) _____ because of the amount of water (4) _____ in the air. The bodies of water present in a swamp usually have almost no (5) _____ . This lack of movement permits the growth of many kinds of plants even within the water. This plant life and the usual lack of any deep (6) _____ , which would permit the passage of boats, greatly restrict travel through the swamp. Although a trip through a swamp can entertain the visitor with the sight of (7) _____ which he will not see in other areas, undoubtedly the inexperienced swamp traveler will feel some (8) _____ at his strange but interesting surroundings.

Follow-up

G. Dictation: Write the sentences that your teacher reads aloud.

1. _____
2. _____
3. _____
4. _____
5. _____

H. Answer the following questions.

1. At what latitude and longitude does this area lie?
2. What type of vegetation is typical here? In your hometown?
3. Describe the typical indications that a storm will let up soon.
4. Are there any unusual weather phenomena in your hometown? Describe them.
5. What do you consider to be a really gloomy day?
6. Can you see the horizon from the outside of this building? Why or why not?
7. Is the air here moist or dry? In your hometown?
8. Are there any swamps in your country? Where?
9. Are there any wooded areas near here? Where?
10. How many television channels can people receive here? Which channel is your favorite?
11. What units of measurement do people in your country use?

I. Complete the story.

John was hiking with some friends in a swamp one day when he got separated from them. . . .

Media (A)

Word Form Chart

NOUN	VERB	ADJECTIVE	ADVERB
		capital	
censor	censor	censored	
censorship			
circulation	circulate	circulated	
		circulating	
contemporary		contemporary	
			fairly
firmness		firm	firmly
focus	focus on	focused	
glance	glance		
	go over		
humility	humble	humble	humbly
		humbling	
interpretation	interpret	interpreted	
interpreter			
mention	mention		
omission	omit	omitted	
	pass on		
	put across		
reaction	react		
sincerity		sincere	sincerely
	touch on		
	turn down		
vagueness		vague	vaguely
version			
write-up	write up		

Definitions and Examples

1. **glance** [to look at something very quickly]

   I **glanced** at the headlines as I stood at the bus stop.
   A quick **glance** at her desk showed her that she had a lot of work to do.

2. **omit** [not to include]

   The news article **omitted** some important details.
   The **omitted** information was an attack on the government.

3. **go over** [to review]

   The reporter from the paper **went over** the story with me carefully.
   This cover **goes over** the computer when it is not in use to protect it from dust.
   The police **went over** the clues again and again to try to discover more information about the killer.
   This article **goes over** the basis of the problem.

4. **contemporary** (a) [of the current time period]

   The story is a **contemporary** one—it occurs in the second half of the twentieth century.
   Contemporary writers are often influenced by writers of the past.

   (b) [a person of about the same age or time]

   The two famous authors were **contemporaries** who spent a lot of time together.
   Professor Michaelson was my **contemporary** at the university.

5. **sincere** [honest]

   He seemed **sincere**, but I did not know whether to trust him.
   The man was **sincerely** sorry that his car had struck the little girl.

6. **capital** (a) [large {used only to describe letters in writing}]

   You should begin each sentence with a **capital** letter.
   Some people use only **capital** letters when they print.

   (b) [2-11: the city where the government of a state or country is located]

   Washington, D.C., is the **capital** of the United States.

7. **humble** (a) [not big, expensive, or important]

   He has a **humble** job with the government and does not have any power.

   (b) [not proud; modest]

   She is very **humble** and never talks about her achievements.
   I **humbly** ask for your forgiveness.

8. **pass on** {separable} [to give to someone]

> The employee **passed on** the suggestion to her supervisor.
> If you have any ideas about who committed the crime, you should **pass** them **on** to the police.
> When you finish the book, **pass** it **on** to a friend.

9. **put across** {separable} [to explain adequately]

> That article **puts across** its main points well.
> The speaker had several interesting ideas, but he did not **put** them **across** effectively.

10. **censor** [to force someone to omit some part of a written or spoken communication]

> The press in some countries is severely **censored**; it is not permitted to print articles against government policies.
> Many people are against all forms of **censorship**; they believe that there should be no restrictions on the media.
> Her letter had been **censored**, and some of the words were blacked out.

11. **circulation** [the average number of copies of a publication sold during a time period]

> The magazine with the largest **circulation** in the United States is TV Guide.

12. **circulate** [to flow; to move around]

> The blood **circulates** through the body.
> That news is **circulating** all over town.
> The party's host **circulated** among his guests.

13. **mention** [to say something in a small way]

> The article **mentioned** my name twice.
> In the government report no **mention** was made of the crisis.
> Please do not even **mention** that topic to my grandmother, or she will get angry.

14. **touch on** [to mention]

> The article **touched on** that idea but did not explain it in depth.
> The president's speech **touched on** a variety of topics but was mainly concerned with the war.

15. vague [not specific]

> That article was quite **vague**; it mentioned hardly any specific information.
>
> If you try to talk about something that you do not know much about, your speech will be too **vague**.

16. write up {separable} [to take information and put it into a connected written form]

> The reporter **wrote up** the story from his notes.
>
> In chemistry lab, we have to **write up** each of our experiments after their completion. Sometimes it takes less time to do the experiment than to **write** it **up**.
>
> Her **write-up** of the information was over ten pages long.

17. version [a form of a type or original]

> I prefer the movie **version** of that book.
>
> There are many **versions** of the Bible in English, but the most popular one was translated in the seventeenth century.

18. fairly (a) [quite]

> These two versions of that play are **fairly** similar; there are very few differences between them.

(b) [adequately]

> The students thought the lecture was **fairly** good, but they had expected it to be much better.

    (c) **fair** [4-1: with equal consideration to all]

>   A good professor must be **fair** to all students.

19. firm (a) [not weak or uncertain]

> The president's voice was **firm** during his speech; he left no room for arguments.
>
> When you shake a person's hand, you should do so **firmly**.

(b) [not soft]

> It is important to build a house on **firm** ground.
>
> I like to sleep on a **firm** bed; if it is too soft, I get a backache.

20. focus (on) (a) [a center of activity, attraction, or attention]

> The **focus** of the article was on possible solutions to the problem.
>
> The professor told us to be sure that our papers **focused on** only one aspect of the issue.

(b) [to adjust a camera to clearness]

> He spent a moment **focusing** the camera and then took the picture.

21. **interpret** [to explain or tell the meaning of]

> After the president gives a speech, the media try to **interpret** exactly what each sentence means.
> If you go to a country where you do not speak the language, you may need an **interpreter**.

22. **reaction** [an action or condition which follows and is caused by another action]

> The population's **reaction** to the president's speech was favorable.
> As a **reaction** against the recent increase in crime, some people have begun to carry weapons.

23. **turn down** {separable} [to refuse]

> The newspaper wanted to publish her story, but she **turned** them **down**.
> Few reporters would **turn down** the opportunity to interview the president.

24. **figure** (a) [a shape or form drawn to help explain something]

> Articles in scientific journals often contain many **figures** which help explain their main point.

> (b) [2-24: a number]

> A mathematician works with **figures**.

Introductory Exercises

A. Match each word with its definition.

_____ 1. to cover or review

_____ 2. to explain adequately

_____ 3. honest

_____ 4. not specific

_____ 5. to say something in a small way

_____ 6. quite

_____ 7. to mention

_____ 8. a form of a type or original

_____ 9. to explain or tell the meaning of

_____ 10. to refuse

_____ 11. the average number of copies of a publication sold during a time period

_____ 12. large (used only to describe letters)

_____ 13. to look at something very quickly

_____ 14. to force someone to omit some part of a written or spoken communication

_____ 15. not to include

_____ 16. of the current time period

_____ 17. to give someone (information)

_____ 18. to take information and put it into a connected written form

_____ 19. not weak or uncertain

_____ 20. a center of activity, attraction or attention

_____ 21. an action or condition which follows and is caused by another action

a. capital
b. censor
c. circulation
d. contemporary
e. fairly
f. firm
g. focus
h. glance
i. go over
j. humble
k. interpret
l. mention
m. omit
n. pass on
o. put across
p. reaction
q. sincere
r. touch on
s. turn down
t. vague
u. version
v. write up

B. Answer each question with a word from the word form chart.

1. What do students do with the information which they gather in a lab experiment?
2. What do people do with job offers that they don't want to accept?
3. Name an action done with the eyes.
4. What do many governments do to information that they don't like?
5. What job can you do if you know two languages well?
6. How does a very honest person speak?
7. How does a person speak if he doesn't know enough about his topic?

8. What does the blood do in the body?
9. What should you do with information that someone else needs?
10. What does a speaker hope to do with his main ideas?
11. What do the citizens do to a new government policy?
12. What do we call art that has been produced recently?

Study Exercises

C. Write **T** if the sentence is true and **F** if it is false.

_____ 1. A sincere person often lies.

_____ 2. A glance is a quick look at something.

_____ 3. Newspaper and magazine publishers want a large circulation.

_____ 4. An interpreter tries to put across someone else's ideas.

_____ 5. The focus of an article is usually a small detail.

_____ 6. It is good to omit important things when you write a report.

_____ 7. Governments censor ideas that they like.

_____ 8. Most of the letters in an English sentence should be capital ones.

_____ 9. Humble people do not talk about their own achievements.

_____ 10. If you do not understand something you have read, you should go over it again.

_____ 11. Something which is contemporary was created recently.

_____ 12. Vague articles in the newspaper give a lot of detailed information.

_____ 13. People want their elected leaders to be firm in their actions.

_____ 14. Good speakers put across their ideas clearly.

D. Match each word with its opposite.

_____ 1. contemporary

_____ 2. firm

_____ 3. glance

_____ 4. humble

_____ 5. omit

_____ 6. keep

_____ 7. sincere

_____ 8. turn down

_____ 9. vague

a. weak
b. pass on
c. proud
d. dishonest
e. focus on
f. old
g. accept
h. include
i. new
j. specific
k. examine

E. Match each two-word verb with its definition.

_____ 1. blow over	**a.** to become
_____ 2. clear up	**b.** to give to someone
_____ 3. go over	**c.** to refuse
_____ 4. let up	**d.** to wash the surface of something
_____ 5. pass on	**e.** to become less severe
_____ 6. put across	**f.** to mention
_____ 7. touch on	**g.** to take information and put it into a connected written form
_____ 8. turn down	**h.** to explain adequately
_____ 9. turn into	**i.** to accept
_____ 10. wash off	**j.** to become clear
_____ 11. write up	**k.** to go away without causing any problem
	l. to review

F. In each blank, write the most appropriate word from the word form chart.

The popularity of a newspaper or magazine depends on a variety of factors. When a potential reader initially (1) _____ at the publication, he needs to be able to see its focus easily. When he (2) _____ its content more carefully, he will want to see that the publication's information is (3) _____ clearly. If the facts are (4) _____ in a way that appears vague, the reader's (5) _____ to the publication will be negative. Readers also want to get all the facts concerning a given situation. Thus, if an article obviously (6) _____ important information, either because of poor writing or intentional (7) _____ , readers will not be pleased. In addition to simply reporting all the facts, the writing of most news articles includes at least some (8) _____ of what those facts mean. This explanation also needs to be accurate and complete. In summary, publications which are well written and which (9) _____ information which the people need and want will have a large (10) _____ .

Follow-up

G. Answer the following questions.

1. Under what political conditions is censorship usually the most severe? Why?
2. Who is your favorite contemporary writer? Why?
3. If you are trying to memorize a page of information, how many times do you need to go over it?
4. Describe someone you know or know about who is humble. Is humility a respected characteristic in your culture?
5. Where can interpreters in your country find work?
6. Under what circumstances should a reporter omit information from a news article?
7. How can a public speaker put his ideas across most effectively?
8. What are some ways that citizens can show their reaction to a new government policy?
9. How can you judge if a person is sincere or not?
10. Is being vague ever considered to be a good thing in your country? Under what circumstances?
11. Name something that has more than one version.

Education

Word Form Chart

NOUN	VERB	ADJECTIVE	ADVERB
anthropologist			
anthropology		anthropological	anthropologically
apparatus			
	catch on		
	catch up		
competence		competent	competently
incompetence		incompetent	incompetently
drill	drill		
dropout	drop out		
economics		economic	
economy	economize	economical	economically
evaluation	evaluate	evaluated	
	fall behind		
foundation	found	founding	
founder			
fulfillment	fulfill	fulfilling	
		fulfilled	
handout	hand out		
hose			
means			
participation	participate	participating	
participant			
preference	prefer	preferred	
		preferential	preferentially
race		racial	racially
ratio			
rubber		rubber	
		rubbery	

NOUN	VERB	ADJECTIVE	ADVERB
sort	sort	sorted	
		sorting	
submission	submit	submitted	
		submissive	submissively
tenure		tenured	
thesis			

Definitions and Examples

1. **found** [to establish]

   That college was **founded** in 1859.
   The town is named for its **founders**.

2. **foundation** (a) [the basis; the basic part; the part at the bottom]

   My physics book is called **Foundations** of Physics; it covers all the basic theories.
   The **foundation** of that building is weak; it may fall down.

   (b) [an organization established with money so that it may continue into the future]

   Her tuition is paid for by a scholarship from a private **foundation**.
   The research of scientists is often supported by money from **foundations**.

3. **apparatus** {plural: apparatus or apparatuses} [equipment]

   We need a new piece of **apparatus** for the experiment we plan to do next.
   That truck has a special **apparatus** on the back for pulling cars out of the snow.

4. **competent** [able to accomplish a particular job; well qualified or well trained]

   That foundation is looking for **competent** biologists to give research money to.
   Incompetent doctors can kill people and should not be permitted to practice medicine.

5. **fulfill** [to complete (a requirement)]

   Researchers who want to get money from a foundation must **fulfill a** variety of requirements.
   It is impossible to **fulfill** the graduation requirements at that college in less than three years.

6. **fulfilling** [satisfying]

   Her job at the hospital does not pay much, but she finds it very **fulfilling** to help people.

7. **evaluate** [to judge how good or how bad someone or something is]

> Tests are used to **evaluate** students' progress in school.
> After **evaluating** the patient's condition, the doctor decided to try the new drug.

8. **sort** (a) [a type; a kind]

> He is the **sort** of person who is always serious.
>
> A: What **sort** of school do you want?
> B: I'm looking for a two-year junior college.

(b) [to classify into groups or categories]

> A machine in the bakery **sorts** the cookies into broken ones and unbroken ones.

9. **drop out (of)** [to quit school, an organization, an event, etc.]

> Some high school students **drop out** when they turn sixteen.
> He **dropped out of** college when they raised the tuition.
> If you **drop out of** this race, you can't compete in the national races.

10. **drill** (a) [to instruct by using repetitive exercises]

> The teacher **drills** us each day on the new vocabulary words.
> In elementary school we did many **drills** to learn to rapidly multiply numbers in our heads.

> (b) [3-6: a tool which makes holes by moving rapidly in a circle]

> The dentist used a **drill** on my bad tooth.

11. **catch on (to)** (a) [to understand]

> I am not good at math; it takes me a while to **catch on** when the teacher shows us a new sort of problem.
> You will **catch on to** this fast if you listen carefully.

(b) [become popular]

> That new restaurant has really **caught on**; it is crowded every evening.
> Some new fashions **catch on** quickly, but others never become popular.

12. **catch up (with/to)** [to reach the level of others who have done more than you have]

> After I was sick for a week, I had trouble **catching up** in my Spanish class.
> He could not **catch up with** the lead runner, so he lost the race.

13. **fall behind (in)** [to go slower than others and so not accomplish as much as they do after starting at the same level]

> I fell **behind in** my studies when I was ill; now I have to catch up if I want to graduate with my class.
> She fell **behind** the rest of her class and was unable to catch up.

14. **rubber** [a substance made from the dried milky juices of various tropical plants]

> Tires on cars and bicycles are usually made of **rubber**.
> **Rubber** bends and stretches easily.

15. **hose** [a flexible, long, thin, rope-shaped object through which liquids or gases can flow]

> We used a **hose** to wash our car.
> A lot of rubber **hose** is used in the laboratory to connect various parts of our apparatus.
> Firemen use very large water **hoses** to fight fires.

16. **prefer** [to like better]

> I **prefer** to have most of my college classes in the morning; then I can study in the afternoon.

> A: Would you **prefer** coffee or tea?
> B: I'll take tea, please.

17. **race** (a) [a division of mankind possessing characteristics that are inherited and sufficiently different to characterize it as a specific human type]

> Africa was originally populated by members of the black **race**.
> When Europeans first saw the American Indians in the fifteenth century, they did not know if they were human because they were a different **race**.
> Relations between the **races** in the United States have improved during the last twenty years.

> > (b) [2-14: a competition]

> > She won the **race** because she ran the fastest.

18. **anthropology** [the study of man, especially his origin, classification, environmental and social relations, and culture]

> In **anthropology** class, we learned about how early man lived.
> **Anthropologists** have classified humans into a variety of racial categories.

19. **tenure** [the act or right of holding something, particularly a position, such as a teaching job]

> After a teacher receives **tenure**, he or she cannot easily be dismissed from his or her job.
> About 60% of the professors in the anthropology department are **tenured**.

20. **economics** [the study of the production, distribution, and use of goods and services in societies]

> That **economics** professor is doing research on the causes of unemployment.

21. **economy** [the system of the production, distribution, and use of goods and services in a society]

> The **economy** of that country is strong; there is almost no unemployment.
> The state of the **economy** will be an important election issue.
> This is an **economic** question, not a political one.

22. **economical** [saving money; not wasteful]

> The new type of car is very **economical** on gas.

23. **economize** [to reduce costs or spending]

> They **economized** by turning the heat down and using fewer lights.

24. **thesis** {plural: theses} (a) [an idea or point which a person agrees with and argues for, especially in a scholarly situation]

> The **thesis** of his paper was that Spanish and Italian are more closely related than Spanish and Portuguese.
> The professor did not like my paper; he said that I did not adequately prove my **thesis**.

(b) [a long, involved paper, usually a requirement for graduate school]

> Her **thesis** was about the effects of imports on the local economy.

25. **means** {always plural} [something useful or helpful to reach a goal; method]

> Some reporters will use any **means** available to get a good story.
> The law does not permit people to keep money that they got through illegal **means**.

26. **mean** (a) [occupying a middle position; average]

> To find the **mean** of five numbers, add them together, and then divide by five.

(b) [not nice; unkind]

> The child thought that his mother was **mean** because she made him go to bed early.

(c) [assumed: to show; to indicate]

> In mathematics, the "mean" **means** the "average."

27. **participate (in)** [to have a part in an organized activity]

> In high school she **participated in** several sports.
> We are expected to **participate** actively in French class.

28. **ratio** [the relationship in quantity, amount, or size between two or more things]

>   The **ratio** of workers to available jobs in that city is too high; many people are unemployed.
>   The **ratio** of water to flour in this cake is too low; it is very dry.
>   There is a very low teacher-student **ratio** at that college. Each teacher has no more than fifteen students in a class.

29. **submit** [to give (something) to an authority]

>   We have to **submit** our research papers no later than December 18.
>   She **submitted** applications to eleven companies, but she may not be hired by any of them.

30. **submit (to)** [to surrender to someone's authority]

>   If the editors want to continue publishing the newspaper, they will have to **submit to** government censorship.

31. **submissive** [surrendering easily to others]

>   That child is very **submissive**; he always does whatever the other children want him to do.

32. **hand out (to)** {separable} [to distribute]

>   The teacher **handed** the exam papers **out to** the students.
>   After the flood, the Red Cross **handed out** food and blankets **to** the victims.

Introductory Exercises

A.   Match each word with its definition.

_____	**1.**	a type; a kind
_____	**2.**	to give (something) to an authority
_____	**3.**	a substance made from the dried milky juices of various tropical plants
_____	**4.**	to understand
_____	**5.**	the system of the production, distribution, and use of goods and services in a society
_____	**6.**	the act or right of holding something, especially a teaching job
_____	**7.**	to have a part in an organized activity
_____	**8.**	to judge how good or bad someone or something is
_____	**9.**	able to accomplish a particular job
_____	**10.**	equipment
_____	**11.**	to distribute
_____	**12.**	to establish
_____	**13.**	to complete (a requirement)
_____	**14.**	something useful or helpful to reach a goal
_____	**15.**	a position which a person holds and argues for, especially in a scholarly situation
_____	**16.**	a flexible, long, thin, rope-shaped object through which liquids or gases can flow
_____	**17.**	to like better
_____	**18.**	the study of man
_____	**19.**	to reach the level of others who have done more than you have
_____	**20.**	to instruct by using repetitive exercises
_____	**21.**	to quit (school, a contest, or an organization)
_____	**22.**	the relationship in quantity, amount, or size between two or more things
_____	**23.**	to go slower than others and so not accomplish as much as they do after starting at the same level

a. anthropology
b. apparatus
c. catch on (to)
d. catch up (with)
e. competent
f. drill
g. drop out (of)
h. economy
i. evaluate
j. fall behind
k. found
l. fulfill
m. hand out (to)
n. hose
o. means
p. participate
q. prefer
r. race
s. ratio
t. rubber
u. sort
v. submit
w. tenure
x. thesis

B. Answer each question with a word from the word form chart.

1. What can a hose be made of?
2. What is at the bottom of a house?
3. What do you need in a laboratory?
4. What do teachers want to get?
5. What will you do if you don't study?
6. What can you do to memorize something?
7. How do you describe someone who can't do his job?
8. What might you use when you wash a car?
9. What should you do after you fall behind in class?
10. What should you do with requirements?
11. What should you study if you want to understand the price of things?
12. What do you do with an application?
13. What is "twenty to one" an example of?
14. Who might go to an isolated island and study the culture of the people there?
15. What is the thing you like best?
16. What is one difference between Africans and Asians?

Study Exercises

C. Write **T** if the sentence is true and **F** if it is false.

_____ 1. Submissive people make good leaders.

_____ 2. The evaluation of a student who catches on quickly will probably be good.

_____ 3. People with fulfilling jobs like their work.

_____ 4. Stamp collectors must sort the stamps they get.

_____ 5. People prefer rubbery beef to other sorts of beef.

_____ 6. Elementary school students write theses.

_____ 7. Schools prefer to give incompetent teachers tenure.

_____ 8. There are only two races on Earth.

_____ 9. Many universities have anthropology and economics departments.

_____ 10. Foundations help students by giving them money.

_____ 11. If you no longer want to participate in something, you can sometimes drop out of it.

_____ 12. All teachers need apparatus to drill in a classroom.

D. Choose the most appropriate two- or three-word verb, and write its correct form in the blank. The sentences are all part of the same story.

1. During the past month, my economics professor has been
   _____ a lot of theories.
   a. catch on   **b.** hand out   **c.** go over

2. For each theory, he has _____ some written notes to us.
   a. touch on   **b.** hand out   **c.** drop

3. After one more month, we will have to _____ a paper about these theories.
   a. catch on   **b.** touch on   **c.** write up

4. The professor will evaluate our papers on how well we _____ our ideas.
   a. put across   **b.** hand out   **c.** touch on

5. Unfortunately, I have been absent too many times during the past month
   and have _____ in the class.
   a. fall behind   **b.** turn down   **c.** pass on

6. I have missed so many lectures that I do not see how I can
   _____ now.
   a. catch on   **b.** catch up   **c.** turn down

7. I went to the professor this week and asked him if I could
   _____ the class.
   a. pass on   **b.** drop out   **c.** drop out of

8. But he _____ my request and said that I had to finish the course.
   a. catch on   **b.** pass on   **c.** turn down

E. In each blank, write the most appropriate word from the word form chart.

In American universities, one of the major requirements for completing graduate-level studies is usually a written thesis. In order to (1) _____ this requirement, a student must (2) _____ a lengthy paper in his subject. Departments evaluate their graduate students in a variety of ways, but in most departments the most important (3) _____ of deciding if a student is (4) _____ in his or her subject is the thesis. The thesis must normally represent original research on the part of the student and so is a difficult requirement. In fact, the (5) _____ of the number of students who successfully complete a thesis to the number who begin graduate work is quite small. In other words, many students (6) _____ graduate school before completing their thesis. Because completing the thesis involves original research and doing such research requires a good (7) _____ in one's subject, departments (8) _____ to admit only those students who have demonstrated a good basic knowledge of their subject.

Follow-up

F. Dictation: Write the sentences that your teacher reads aloud.

1. _____
2. _____
3. _____
4. _____
5. _____

G. Answer the following questions.

1. What do you sometimes use hoses for?
2. How do you catch up when you get behind in a class?
3. What percentage of students in your country drops out of school before graduating from high school? Why do they drop out?
4. How are students applying to college in your country evaluated?
5. When was this school founded? By whom?
6. What sports or clubs do you participate in?
7. What is the ratio of men to women in your country?
8. What do you have that is made of rubber?
9. Do you collect anything? How do you sort the items in your collection? According to what criteria?
10. Can high school teachers in your country be tenured? University professors? How long must they teach before receiving tenure? What requirements must a teacher fulfill to receive tenure?

H. Would you prefer to study anthropology or economics? Why?

Housing

Word Form Chart

NOUN	VERB	ADJECTIVE	ADVERB
abandonment	abandon	abandoned	
access		accessible	accessibly
affluence		affluent	affluently
attic			
bargain	bargain	bargaining	
breakdown	break down	broken down	
capital			
	clean off	cleaned off	
	clean out	cleaned out	
	clean up	cleaned up	
dwelling	dwell	dwelling	
dweller			
	dwell on		
enlargement	enlarge	enlarged	
	fix up	fixed up	
installation	install	installed	
insulation	insulate	insulated	
medium			
plumber			
plumbing			
rust	rust	rusty	
sewer			
sewage			
	settle on		
shortage			
site	situate		
structure	structure	structured	
		structural	structurally
transparency		transparent	

Definitions and Examples

1. **shortage** [a lack of something]

    During the war, there was a **shortage** of food, and many people were hungry.

    There is a **shortage** of storage space in my apartment because it is so small.

2. **affluent** [rich; well-supplied with money and possessions]

    That neighborhood is quite **affluent**; all the houses are large.

    Affluence does not always bring happiness.

3. **enlarge** [to make bigger]

    I want to **enlarge** my closet so that I will have space for my clothes.

    We had to **enlarge** our garage when we got a second car.

4. **dwelling** [a building, or part of a building, to live in]

    This neighborhood is filled with single-family **dwellings.**

    His **dwelling** is on the edge of town.

    Some of the American Indians were cave-**dwellers**.

5. **dwell on** [to think about something a lot or too much]

    You should not **dwell on** the death of your brother.

6. **capital** (a) [money and possessions]

    My landlord wants to buy another building, but he does not have enough **capital**.

    That man is very affluent. Between his bank accounts and his possessions, he has a lot of **capital**.

    (b) [**3-11**: the city where a state or national government is located]

    London is the **capital** of England.

    (c) [**5-4**: large (used only concerning letters in writing)]

    You should begin your name with a **capital** letter.

7. **break down** [to stop working; to become broken; to be in bad condition]

    The car **broke down** and we were stuck on a country road all night.

    The house looks old and **broken down**.

8. **fix up** {separable} [to repair; to make nicer]

    They need to **fix up** the outside of their house. It is a mess now, but **fixing** it **up** will cost a lot.

    She **fixed up** that old car and then sold it at a profit.

9. **medium** [in the middle between small and large; average]

   They have a **medium**-sized house in an average neighborhood.

   A: What size sweater do you wear?
   B: **Medium**, usually.

10. **access** [the permission or ability to enter, approach, or communicate with]

    The people living in these apartments have **access** to that swimming pool for free.
    This neighborhood has easy **access** to a variety of stores.

11. **bargain** [to negotiate the terms of an agreement]

    We **bargained** with the agent for two weeks before buying our house.
    You have to **bargain** to get a good price when you buy a car in the United States.

12. **install** [to establish a person or piece of machinery in its proper place]

    We cannot use our new dishwasher until it is properly **installed**.
    The workers who **install** air-conditioning systems are very busy each spring.
    The club will **install** its new officers next week.

13. **insulate** [to isolate something so that it will not leak heat, electricity, or sound]

    We need to **insulate** our house better so that our heating bills will not be so high.
    We can put **insulation** around the doors and windows.
    Rubber is frequently used as an **insulator** on wires that carry electricity.

14. **attic** [a room or space directly below the roof of a building]

    We use our **attic** for storage space.
    You should put insulation in your **attic**.

15. **plumber** [a person who installs and repairs the water pipes in buildings]

    We need a **plumber** to install our new washing machine.
    The **plumbing** in that old house needs a lot of repairs.

16. **rust** [the reddish covering which occurs on iron, especially when the iron is surrounded by moist air]

    The plumber said that all of our pipes are so **rusty** that we should replace them.
    My old car has a lot of **rust**. It needs to be repaired and painted.

17. **sewer** [an underground pipe to carry away waste water and sometimes excess rain water]

> Houses in the city are usually connected to the **sewer** system, which carries the **sewage** to a treatment plant.
> Some poor countries have only open **sewers**, which are not healthy.

18. **settle on** [to decide on]

> We looked at a hundred houses before we **settled on** this one.
> They **settled on** tomorrow as moving day.

19. **site** [the location of an actual or planned building or activity]

> That is the **site** of my grandparents' house, which burned down ten years ago.
> There are many Revolutionary War battle **sites** in New England.

20. **structure** [something, such as a building, which is constructed]

> The tallest **structure** in town is that office building.
> You need to get a building permit from the city government before you begin building any **structure**.
> That bridge is **structurally** weak; it may fall down.

21. **transparent** [clear, able to be seen through]

> Most glass is **transparent**.
> He is very **transparent**. When he lies, I always know that he is lying.

22. **clean off** {separable} [to clean a surface]

> You should **clean off** the table after each meal.
> We have to **clean** the snow **off** the car before we can leave.

23. **clean out** {separable} [to clean a three-dimensional space]

> I have to **clean out** the drawers in my desk. I cannot find anything in them anymore.
> If we **clean out** the basement, we may find some useful tools.
> I am too tired to **clean** it **out** now.

24. **clean up** {separable} [to clean a large three-dimensional space]

> The mayor wants everyone to **clean up** the city before the New Year's celebration.
> Everyone thinks that it will take too much time and money to **clean** it **up** so quickly.
> My mother always **cleans up** the house before guests arrive.

25. **abandon** (a) [to cease maintaining, practicing, or using]

   The **abandoned** building has been vacant for years.
   They **abandoned** those production methods in favor of more economical ones.

   (b) [to stop supporting, protecting, or helping]

   It is against the law for parents to **abandon** their children.

Introductory Exercises

A. Match each word or phrase with its definition.

_____ **1.** rich

_____ **2.** to repair; to make nicer

_____ **3.** money and possessions

_____ **4.** a place to live

_____ **5.** in the middle between small and large

_____ **6.** to stop working; to become broken

_____ **7.** a lack of something

_____ **8.** one who installs and repairs the water pipes in a building

_____ **9.** to decide on

_____ **10.** to negotiate the terms of an agreement

_____ **11.** the location of an actual or planned building or activity

_____ **12.** to establish a person or piece of machinery in its proper place

_____ **13.** the permission or ability to enter, approach, or communicate with

_____ **14.** to isolate something so that it will not leak heat, electricity, or sound

_____ **15.** to make bigger

_____ **16.** a room or space directly below the roof of a building

_____ **17.** to cease maintaining, practicing, or using

_____ **18.** clear; able to be seen through

_____ **19.** to clean a surface

_____ **20.** the system of water pipes in a building

_____ **21.** something, such as a building, which is constructed

_____ **22.** the reddish covering which occurs on iron

a. abandon
b. access
c. affluent
d. attic
e. bargain
f. break down
g. capital
h. clean off
i. clean out
j. clean up
k. dwelling
l. enlarge
m. fix up
n. install
o. insulate
p. medium
q. plumber
r. plumbing
s. rust
t. sewer
u. settle on
v. shortage
w. site
x. structure
y. transparent

B.   Answer each question with a word from the word form chart.

1. What is your house or apartment an example of?
2. What do you need to start a new business?
3. What are houses and bridges examples of?
4. Who should you call if your water won't work?
5. What size is not big and not small?
6. What damages iron?
7. What can help keep your house warm in the winter?
8. What part of a house is near the top?
9. What are under the streets of a city?
10. What do you do to get a good price on something?
11. What can you do if your house is too small?
12. What happens to machinery that is too old?
13. What should you do to your house if it's in bad condition?
14. How can you describe glass?

Study Exercises

C.   Write **T** if the sentence is true and **F** if it is false.

_____ 1. During a shortage, people do not have enough of something.

_____ 2. Affluent people need more money.

_____ 3. The installation of a piece of machinery often requires tools.

_____ 4. The attic in a house is downstairs.

_____ 5. Sewers are usually above the ground.

_____ 6. Moisture makes iron get rusty more quickly than dry air.

_____ 7. An abandoned building is a dwelling for several families.

_____ 8. People want to have sewer systems attached to their homes.

_____ 9. The site of a building is the view from that building.

_____ 10. When a person bargains, he has to pay more money.

_____ 11. Plumbers do most of their work in attics.

_____ 12. You can see through transparent things.

_____ 13. A house with very thin walls has a lot of insulation.

_____ 14. If you have access to something, you can get it.

_____ 15. When something is broken down, it needs to be fixed.

D. Write the letter of each possible object in front of each of the verb phrases. Some of the objects can follow more than one of the verb phrases.

---- **1.** clean off

---- **2.** clean out

---- **3.** clean up

a. a drawer
b. a desk top
c. a television
d. a purse
e. a town
f. a yard
g. the inside of a car
h. the windows of a car
i. a room
j. a stove
k. an oven
l. a sidewalk

E. Match each word with its opposite.

---- **1.** affluence

---- **2.** attic

---- **3.** enlarge

---- **4.** fix up

---- **5.** install

---- **6.** settle on

---- **7.** shortage

a. decrease
b. remove
c. insulate
d. basement
e. argue about
f. poverty
g. hidden
h. access
i. break
j. accumulation

F. In each blank, write the most appropriate word or phrase from the word form chart.

With the prices of newer dwellings continually rising, many young Americans are choosing to buy older homes. However, many of these older houses are not in good condition and require a lot of work. Since the work necessary to (1) _____ a broken-down old house is often expensive, when making such a purchase buyers should be careful that they possess the necessary (2) _____ to complete the repairs. There is a variety of typical expenses. Often experts must be hired; for example, a (3) _____ to replace (4) _____ pipes which are no longer in working condition. Older houses may have been abandoned before the city (5) _____ system was completed, so the new owner must pay to have (6) _____ to that system. Of course, the entire house, from the basement to the (7) _____ , will need to be

(8) _____ . Although newer homes often come supplied with refrigerators and dishwashers, the buyer of an older home will have to pay not only for the purchase of these modern conveniences but also for their (9) _____ . Older homes built when heating costs were low will need to be (10) _____ so that the owners' fuel bills will not be too high. Obviously, there are many costs involved in buying an "inexpensive" older home. However, new owners can keep the costs down by doing much of the work themselves. As long as the (11) _____ of low-cost new homes continues, many Americans who do not mind spending some time and effort fixing up older homes will continue to buy them.

Follow-up

G. Dictation: Write the sentences that your teacher reads aloud.

1. _____
2. _____
3. _____
4. _____
5. _____

H. Answer the following questions.

1. Where do the most affluent people in your country live?
2. For what things do people bargain in your country?
3. Has anything that you own broken down recently? What?
4. Who cleans off the table after you have dinner?
5. In your home what needed to be installed? Who did the installation?
6. Is insulation used in homes in your country? Explain.
7. What size sweater do you wear?
8. What percentage of the homes in your city are connected to sewers?
9. Name some things that you own that may get rusty.
10. Name some things that are transparent.
11. Have there been any shortages in your country? Explain.
12. Do people in your country often buy old houses and fix them up?

I. Describe the most popular types of dwellings in your country.

Farming

Word Form Chart

NOUN	VERB	ADJECTIVE	ADVERB
acre			
acreage			
calf			
	carry on		
drain	drain	drained	
drainage			
earth		earthen	
failure	fail to		
folk			
	get by		
hardship			
harvest	harvest	harvested	
livestock			
	look after		
	look back on		
	nurse	nursing	
persistence	persist	persistent	persistently
pump	pump	pumping	
region		regional	regionally
	run off		
scattering	scatter	scattering	
		scattered	
tractor			
veterinarian		veterinary	
	work out		
yield	yield		

Definitions and Examples

1. **calf** {plural: calves} [a baby cow]

    Calves are often born in the spring.
    Cows usually have only one **calf** at a time.

2. **hardship** [a difficulty]

    Poverty causes many **hardships** for people.
    Having to work 365 days a year is only one of the **hardships** that farmers face.

3. **region** [an area]

    The **region** in the north central area of the United States has a lot of dairy farms.
    The farms in desert **regions** must have irrigation systems because these areas do not get much rain.
    That kind of apple is a **regional** specialty there.

4. **acre** [a unit of land area used in the United States and England equal to 4,047 square meters]

    Our house in the suburbs sits on one **acre** of land.

    A: What is the **acreage** of your ranch?
    B: About 2,000 **acres**.

5. **persist** [to continue to do something although some hardship is in the way]

    He **persisted** in farming although a flood destroyed his crops last year.
    The region along the Mississippi River has a **persistent** problem with flooding.

6. **nurse** (a) [to feed milk to a baby from the mother's body]

    The mother cow **nurses** her calf whenever he is hungry.
    Many American mothers have returned to the custom of **nursing** their babies instead of bottle feeding them.

    (b) [**1-14**: a person, similar to a doctor, but with less training, who gives medical treatment to sick or injured people]

    The **nurses** in a hospital always wear white.

7. **run off** [for a liquid to move away from a specific location]

    The excess rainwater **runs off** the fields and into the pond.
    The water **runs off** the roof and settles in the backyard.

8. **run off** {separable} [to scare someone or something away by chasing it]

    We need to find a way to **run** those wild horses **off** our ranch.
    The farmer **ran off** the boys who were stealing apples.

9. **drain** (away, off) (a) [for water or another liquid to be removed from a place]

    Farmers must construct their fields so that the extra rainwater will **drain** off them.

    (b) [a pipe through which water is taken away]

    The **drain** in our kitchen sink is not working well; the sink is full of water.

10. **drainage** (a) [the act or process of draining]

    After the flood, the **drainage** of that region took two weeks.

    (b) [something drained]

    The **drainage** from storms goes into the storm sewers.

11. **earth** (a) [the soil]

    Crops grow well in this region because the **earth** is rich.
    This **earth** is still damp from last night's rain.

    (b) [**1-23**: the planet which we live on]

    The **earth** is the third planet from the sun.

12. **fail to** [to not do something]

    His crops died because he **failed to** irrigate them sufficiently.
    If you **fail to** arrive on time for your appointment, you will not get the job.

13. **folk** (a) [a certain kind or class of people]

    Country **folk** often speak differently from city **folk**.

    (b) [of or from the common people in a region or country]

    My sister likes **folk** music and **folk** dancing.

14. **get by (on)** [to be barely all right (with)]

    I can **get by on** only two meals a day if I have to.
    The farmers are **getting by on** the small amount of rain this summer, but the crops would be healthier with more rain.

15. **harvest** (a) [the act or process of gathering in a crop]

    The farmers are very busy during the **harvest** season.
    Fall is the **harvest** time for many crops.

    (b) [the quantity of a natural product gathered in a single season]

    Last year's **harvest** was a large one, so the farmers are happy.

16. **livestock** [the farm animals raised for use and profit]

> All of the **livestock** on his farm are kept in the barn during the coldest winter days.
> Farmers raise most **livestock**, such as cows and chickens, to eat or to sell for food.
> Sheep are raised as **livestock** for food and for wool.

17. **look after** [to guard; to protect; to care for]

> The older boy **looked after** his little sister while his parents were out.
> His dogs help the farmer **look after** his sheep.

18. **look back on** {separable} [to remember something in the past]

> He often **looks back** happily **on** his childhood.
> You should not **look back on** the sad events in your life.

19. **pump** [a machine that raises or moves a gas or a liquid]

> Irrigation systems use **pumps** to move the water to the field where it is needed.
> The heart **pumps** blood through the body.

20. **scatter** [to distribute irregularly; to throw in all directions]

> The farmer **scattered** seeds on his field at planting time.
> She **scattered** corn on the ground for the chickens to eat.

21. **tractor** [a four-wheeled automotive vehicle used on farms to pull farm machinery]

> The farmer spent all day on his **tractor**, getting the fields ready for planting.
> That **tractor** is pulling a heavy load of hay.

22. **work out** {separable} [to result in a success]

> The farmers hope that the new irrigation project will **work out** well and provide the valley with the water their crops need.
> The problem is difficult, but we hope to **work** it **out** soon.

23. **yield** (a) [to produce as a natural product]

> That field **yields** a larger harvest than this one.
> We should grow this type of wheat because its **yield** per acre is very high.

(b) [to permit another to go first or take your place]

> At the entrance to the highway, you must **yield** to the traffic.

24. **veterinarian** {frequently abbreviated to **vet**} [a doctor who treats animals]

    We need to call the **vet**. One of the horses is sick.
    The **veterinarian** comes to our farm regularly to examine the livestock.

25. **carry on (with)** [to continue (with)]

    The farmer **carried on with** his planting, despite the rain.
    The boss told me to **carry on** after she had checked my work so far.

Introductory Exercises

A. Match each work with its definition.

_____	**1.** an area	**a.** acre
_____	**2.** to be all right	**b.** calf
_____	**3.** the soil	**c.** carry on
_____	**4.** a difficulty	**d.** drain
_____	**5.** to feed milk to a baby from the mother's body	**e.** earth
_____	**6.** a certain kind or class of people	**f.** fail to
_____	**7.** to guard; to protect; to care for	**g.** folk
_____	**8.** the act or process of gathering in a crop	**h.** get by
_____	**9.** a device that raises or moves a gas or a liquid	**i.** hardship
_____	**10.** the farm animals raised for use and profit	**j.** harvest
_____	**11.** to remember something in the past	**k.** livestock
_____	**12.** to distribute irregularly; to throw in all directions	**l.** look after
_____	**13.** to result in a success	**m.** look back on
_____	**14.** to continue to do something although some hardship is in the way	**n.** nurse
_____	**15.** a baby cow	**o.** persist
_____	**16.** a unit of land area	**p.** pump
_____	**17.** for water or liquid to be removed from a place	**q.** region
_____	**18.** a doctor who treats animals	**r.** run off
_____	**19.** to produce as a natural product	**s.** scatter
		t. tractor
		u. veterinarian
		v. work out
		· **w.** yield

B. Answer each question with a word from the word form chart.

1. Who helps sick animals?
2. What happens on a farm in the fall?
3. What is in the bottom of your sink?
4. What is a baby cow?
5. What can you use to get water from underground?
6. What machine does a farmer use?
7. What is another word for "people"?
8. Where do farmers plant seeds?
9. How do farmers measure their land?
10. What is another word for "area"?
11. What do parents do to their children?
12. What are poverty and hunger examples of?
13. What are the animals on a farm?
14. What should you do to achieve a difficult goal?

Study Exercises

C. Write **T** if the sentence is true and **F** if it is false.

_____ 1. Harvesting is the process of planting seeds.

_____ 2. Wheat and rice are examples of livestock.

_____ 3. An acre is a unit of land smaller than a square kilometer and bigger than a square meter.

_____ 4. People usually look back happily on hardships.

_____ 5. Farmers want a high yield from their fields.

_____ 6. A veterinarian often uses a tractor in his work.

_____ 7. If something is scattered, it falls in a variety of places.

_____ 8. People are happy when their problems work out.

_____ 9. Every drain has a pump in it.

_____ 10. Livestock are grown in deep earth.

_____ 11. A persistent person carries on with a job although it is difficult.

_____ 12. Fathers nurse their children every day.

_____ 13. When you fail to achieve a goal, you do not achieve it.

_____ 14. "Folk art" is the art produced by people who have no special training in art.

D.   Complete the analogies with a word from the word form chart.

   1. heart : blood :: _____ : water
   2. pound : meat :: _____ : land
   3. baby : human :: _____ : cow
   4. collection : garbage :: _____ : crops
   5. feed : dog :: _____ : baby
   6. doctor : human :: _____ : livestock
   7. factory : produce :: field : _____
   8. sea : fisherman :: _____ : farmer
   9. insist : words :: _____ : actions
   10. stop : start :: gather : _____

E.   Match each two- or three-word verb with its synonym.

   _____ 1. clean off
   _____ 2. fix up
   _____ 3. settle on
   _____ 4. hand out
   _____ 5. catch on
   _____ 6. go over
   _____ 7. turn down
   _____ 8. carry on
   _____ 9. get by
   _____ 10. look back on
   _____ 11. look after
   _____ 12. work out

   a. distribute
   b. refuse
   c. barely be all right
   d. care for
   e. continue
   f. wash the surface of
   g. remember
   h. scatter
   i. repair
   j. understand
   k. yield
   l. cover
   m. succeed
   n. decide on

F.   In the blanks, write the most appropriate word(s) from the word form chart.

   The summer of 1986 was a difficult one for many American farmers. Some farmers (1) _____ survive the twin problems of low crop prices and lack of rain, but others (2) _____ with help. When these survivors (3) _____ on the events of 1986, they can be proud of their (4) _____ in facing the many (5) _____ which occurred in their lives. Today, most are determined to (6) _____ with farming because they feel that (7) _____ crops and livestock is a satisfying and useful job in

our society. Although the lack of rain during 1986 made the
(8) _____ so dry that the (9) _____ of crops from
most fields was very low, we can hope that things will (10)
_____ better for the American farmers in the future and that the
harvests will be as large as they were before 1986.

Follow-up

G. Dictation: Write the sentences that your teacher reads aloud.

1. _____
2. _____
3. _____
4. _____
5. _____

H. Answer the following questions.

1. How many acres is a typical farm in your country?
2. What folk art or folk music exist in your country?
3. How many times each year can crops be harvested in your country?
4. What kinds of livestock are most typically raised in your country?
5. Do mothers in your country more commonly nurse or bottle-feed their babies? Why?
6. Which region of your country contains the most farmland? Why?
7. By what methods do farmers in your country increase the yield of their fields?
8. Do farmers in your country have trouble getting by on just their crop and livestock yields, or do they need to supplement their incomes? Why?
9. Do parents in your country permit nonfamily members (babysitters) to look after their children? Under what circumstances is this permitted or not permitted?
10. Do farmers in your country commonly use tractors? For what do they use them?

I. Describe some of the duties of a veterinarian in a farming region.

Work

Word Form Chart

NOUN	VERB	ADJECTIVE	ADVERB
absolute		absolute	absolutely
absoluteness			
addict		addicted	
		addictive	
aim	aim	aimless	aimlessly
automation	automate	automatic	automatically
		brief	briefly
	carry out		
collapse	collapse	collapsed	
		collapsing	
		collapsible	
compensation	compensate	compensated	
		compensatory	compensatorily
		crucial	crucially
dedication	dedicate	dedicated	dedicatedly
director	direct	directing	
direction		directed	
	do over		
	fill in		
	fill out		
firm			
form			
garage			
	get on with		
		indispensable	indispensably
	look over		
responsibility		responsible	responsibly
irresponsibility		irresponsible	irresponsibly

NOUN	VERB	ADJECTIVE	ADVERB
screen	screen	screening	
		screened	
		sore	
		subsequent	subsequently
transition		transitional	transitionally

Definitions and Examples

1. **look over** {separable} [to examine; to read]

   My supervisor told me to **look over** this report.
   I **looked** it **over**, but I could not find any errors.

2. **crucial** [very important]

   The next month will be a **crucial** one for our company; we must make a
   large profit, or we will not be able to continue in business.
   I am nervous whenever I have to make a **crucial** decision.

3. **fill in (for)** [to substitute (for)]

   When a worker in the factory is absent, another worker must **fill in for**
   him or her.
   I **filled in for** my brother because he was sick and could not drive the
   truck.

4. **firm** (a) [a company]

   He works for a small **firm** that sells heavy machinery.
   That **firm** is very successful. They are now hiring more salesmen.

   (b) [5-4: not weak or uncertain]

   The president's voice was **firm** during his speech; he left no
   room for arguments.

5. **aim** [a goal; a target]

   His **aim** is to start his own company.
   She **aims** to finish her medical degree in two years.
   When he is angry he walks **aimlessly** through the countryside, not going
   to any special place but just trying to forget his anger.

6. **brief** [not lasting a long time; not long]

   He gets a **brief** vacation each year—only four or five days.
   The professor asked us to write a **brief** report on a current event.

7. **direct** (a) [to control; to manage]

> A foreign engineer is **directing** the irrigation project.
> The **director** of the play is not satisfied yet with our performance.

> > (b) [**3**-5: in the shortest way]

> > > The **direct** route will take us only thirty minutes.

8. **garage** (a) [a place where vehicles are repaired]

> I have to take my car to the **garage** to have it repaired.
> If you cannot fix the engine yourself, you will have to take it to a **garage**.

> > (b) [**1**-12: a small building or a part of a house for storing a car]

> > > We keep our car in the **garage** at night.

9. **do over** {separable} [to repeat (an action)]

> If my supervisor does not like this report, I will have to **do** it **over**.
> He always **does** his work **over** and **over** until it is perfect.

10. **form** (a) [an official paper with blanks to be written on]

> Before the interview, I had to complete a long **form**.
> The government tax **forms** are too long!

> > (b) [**2**-23: the shape of something]

> > > I made a cake in the **form** of the letter T.

> > (c) [**2**-23: a way of doing something]

> > > I saw a group that performs an ancient **form** of dancing.

> > (d) [**2**-23: to make in a certain way]

> > > The students **formed** a group to study for the test.

11. **fill out** {separable} [to complete (a form)]

> He told me to **fill out** the application in pen.
> She **filled** it **out** quickly, but she made too many spelling errors.

12. **responsible** (a) [serious about doing one's job or studies well]

> Employers want **responsible** employees who will do their jobs carefully.
> She is too young to act very **responsibly**.

> > (b) [**2**-11: having control over decisions]

> > > Parents are **responsible** for their children; they must provide food, shelter, and love.

13. **absolutely** (a) [totally; completely; really]

> She is **absolutely** sure that she can do the job.

> (b) [certainly]

> > A: Are you going to try to find a new job?
> > B: Yes. **Absolutely**.

14. **addict** [a person who is physically or mentally dependent upon something]

> Drug **addicts** usually must have medical treatment to be cured.
> She is **addicted** to her work; she works sixteen hours a day and says that she never thinks of anything else.

15. **automatic** (a) [having a self-acting mechanism]

> The **automatic** door opened as we approached it.
> Many American banks have **automatic** money machines so that you can make a withdrawal day or night without talking to a teller.
> Companies **automate** their factories to save labor costs; one machine in some industries can do the work of twenty people.

> (b) [involuntary]

> I **automatically** jump back if I see a snake.

16. **carry out** {separable} [to do]

> You should **carry out** your boss' instructions quickly and carefully.
> The researcher **carried out** the experiment in his lab during the past two months; however, he **carried** it **out** in total secrecy.

17. **collapse** (a) [to fall (said of people)]

> The sick man **collapsed** on the street.
> She **collapsed** from the heat.

> (b) [to fall and be destroyed]

> The bridge **collapsed** and killed several people on it.
> The old building **collapsed** and trapped some people inside.

> (c) [to fold into a smaller shape]

> The telescope **collapsed** into one small piece for easy carrying.
> A **collapsible** chair can be folded and carried easily by one person.

> (d) [to suddenly lose force or effectiveness]

> The efforts toward peace **collapsed** when the city was bombed.

18. **indispensable** [absolutely necessary]

> Her work is **indispensable** to the project; without her we cannot continue.

19. **sore** [painful]

> His back was **sore** from lifting heavy boxes onto the truck.
> I am going to the doctor because I have a **sore** throat.

20. **subsequent** [following; next]

> At the first meeting our boss was angry; at the **subsequent** meeting he listened to our plans.
> First, he was told that his work was very poor; **subsequently,** he was fired.

21. **transition** [change; a movement from one state to another]

> Our company is in **transition**; in the past it was quite small, but now it is growing rapidly.
> The **transition** from being a student to working full-time is a difficult one for many young people.

22. **compensation** [something (often money) given or received in payment for a service or because of an injury]

> The workers are on strike because they feel that they do not receive adequate **compensation** for their labor.
> The insurance company paid him $10,000 in **compensation** after his accident.

23. **dedicated (to)** (a) [very serious about a certain cause, ideal, or purpose]

> She is very **dedicated to** her work; she rarely thinks of anything else.
> I respect his **dedication to** his family.

(b) [assigned to a certain purpose]

> The money collected by the children in the church was **dedicated to** helping the poor.
> The new building is **dedicated to** the memory of the president who died recently.

24. **screen** (a) [to examine methodically in order to separate into groups]

> The candidates for the job were carefully **screened** so that only the best three were interviewed.

(b) [something that protects or hides]

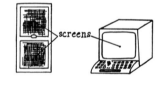

> The **screens** in the windows keep the insects out but let the cool winds in.
> A **screen** separated her bed from the rest of her one-room apartment.

(c) [the flat surface on which a television or movie picture is shown]

> Some of the newer televisions have very large **screens**.
> I used a soft cloth to clean the **screen** of the television.

25. **get on with** [to start; to continue with]

> Let's **get on with** this work, or we will never finish by dinnertime.
> The teacher told me to stop wasting time and **get on with** the assignment.

Introductory Exercises

A. Match each word with its definition.

_____ **1.** to substitute (for)

_____ **2.** to complete (a form)

_____ **3.** totally; complete; really

_____ **4.** painful

_____ **5.** change; a movement from one state to another

_____ **6.** something that protects or hides

_____ **7.** absolutely necessary

_____ **8.** to fall (said of people)

_____ **9.** to control; to manage

_____ **10.** to repeat (an action)

_____ **11.** following; next

_____ **12.** something given or received in payment for a service or because of an injury

_____ **13.** to examine; to read

_____ **14.** very important

_____ **15.** a goal; a target

_____ **16.** an official piece of paper with blanks to be written on

_____ **17.** a company

_____ **18.** not lasting a long time

_____ **19.** serious about doing one's job or studies well; reliable

_____ **20.** a place where vehicles are repaired

_____ **21.** having a self-acting mechanism

_____ **22.** a person who is physically or mentally dependent on something

a. absolutely
b. addict
c. aim
d. automatic
e. brief
f. carry out
g. collapse
h. compensation
i. crucial
j. dedicated
k. direct
l. do over
m. fill in (for)
n. fill out
o. firm
p. form
q. garage
r. get on with
s. indispensable
t. look over
u. responsible
v. screen
w. sore
x. subsequent
y. transition

B. Answer each question with a word from the word form chart.

1. What do people receive for their work?
2. Where can you take your car for repairs?
3. What are movies at a theater shown on?
4. Who is in charge of the making of a movie?
5. What do you fill out for the government?

6. What can happen to people if they don't eat any food for a long time?
7. What is a person who can't stop taking drugs?
8. What do you do with an application form?
9. What does a substitute do?
10. What should you do if you spill coffee on your homework and you can't read it?
11. How can you describe one second?
12. How do you feel after exercising and using muscles that you rarely use?
13. What kind of workers do employers want? (two answers)
14. What do you do with a piece of your writing to find any errors?
15. What do soldiers do before they shoot their guns?

Study Exercises

C. Write **T** if the sentence is true and **F** if it is false.

_____ 1. Dedication and responsibility are good characteristics in an employee.

_____ 2. A person can collapse from hunger.

_____ 3. Workers try to avoid compensation.

_____ 4. A director gives orders.

_____ 5. Someone who is indispensable can be easily replaced.

_____ 6. A transition is a period of no change.

_____ 7. People like to have sore muscles.

_____ 8. People should avoid addictive things.

_____ 9. When you check something, you look it over carefully.

_____ 10. A brief period lasts a long time.

_____ 11. Screens are used for protection.

_____ 12. Crucial events do not have much importance.

_____ 13. An automatic door must be opened by hand.

_____ 14. An action which is subsequent to another action occurs before that action.

_____ 15. People work for firms.

_____ 16. A form is a piece of paper.

D. Match each word with its opposite.

___ **1.** absolutely		**a.** unimportant
___ **2.** automatic		**b.** long
___ **3.** brief		**c.** irresponsible
___ **4.** collapsible		**d.** stop
___ **5.** crucial		**e.** not at all
___ **6.** get on with		**f.** dedicated
___ **7.** responsible		**g.** indispensable
___ **8.** subsequent		**h.** voluntary
		i. previous
		j. firm

E. Match each word with its synonym.

___ **1.** absolutely		**a.** indispensable
___ **2.** aim		**b.** manage
___ **3.** crucial		**c.** continue
___ **4.** direct		**d.** totally
___ **5.** carry out		**e.** examine
___ **6.** do over		**f.** repeat
___ **7.** fill in for		**g.** voluntary
___ **8.** fill out		**h.** complete
___ **9.** get on with		**i.** company
___ **10.** firm		**j.** do
___ **11.** look over		**k.** next
___ **12.** sore		**l.** change
___ **13.** subsequent		**m.** painful
___ **14.** transition		**n.** substitute
		o. goal

F. Circle the word which does not fit.

1. aim for	**a.** a target	**4.** look over	**a.** some homework
	b. a gun		**b.** some work
	c. a goal		**c.** some dinner
2. carry out	**a.** an order	**5.** direct	**a.** a meal
	b. an experiment		**b.** a project
	c. a problem		**c.** a play
3. fill out	**a.** an application	**6.** screen	**a.** some holidays
	b. a form		**b.** some applicants
	c. a book		**c.** some movies

G. In each blank, write the correct form of the two- or three-word verb phrase from the following group which is the most appropriate. More than one answer may be possible.

carry on (with)	run off	fill out
get by (with)	work out	get on with
look back on	carry out	look over
look after	do over	fill in (for)

Last week, the experiment which I worked on did not (1) _____ , so this week I decided to (2) _____ it _____ . The experiment took three days to (3) _____ . I hated to spend another three days after my first failure, but it was an important experiment, and I need good results in order to (4) _____ my work. The first step was to (5) _____ an order form to get the chemicals that I needed from the storage room. The regular worker in the storage room was absent, and the boy who was (6) _____ him had trouble finding what I needed. Finally, he was able to find my required chemicals, and I could (7) _____ my work. Three days later, when I had (8) _____ my calculations, I knew that my experiment had been a success. At that time I could (9) _____ my problems at the beginning of the experiment; I realized that those extra three days were worth the time.

Follow-up

H. Dictation: Write the sentences that your teacher reads aloud.

1. _____
2. _____
3. _____
4. _____
5. _____

I. Answer the following questions.

1. How can an employee show dedication to his firm?
2. Which are the largest firms in your country?
3. Do people in your country use screens in their windows? Why or why not?
4. What type of addictions are common in your country? Why?
5. Have you ever collapsed? Why?
6. What forms do you have to fill out? Why?
7. Is your country in a period of transition now? Explain.

    8. What do you do when you have a sore throat?

    9. What does the education system in your country aim to do?

   10. What kinds of actions or situations can make you automatically angry?

J.   Complete the story.

Yesterday, while John Smith was working at his factory job, he collapsed. . . .

Military

Word Form Chart

NOUN	VERB	ADJECTIVE	ADVERB
arms	arm		
	blow up		
campaign	campaign	campaigning	
conqueror	conquer	conquering	
conquest		conquered	
	die down		
discipline	discipline	disciplinary	
		disciplined	
enlistment	enlist	enlisted	
	flee	fleeing	
	give away		
	give up		
hero		heroic	heroically
heroine			
		junior	
	lay in		
major			
outcome			
rebel	rebel	rebellious	rebelliously
rebellion		rebelling	
resistance	resist	resisting	
retreat	retreat	retreating	
		senior	
struggle	struggle	struggling	
	tie up	tied up	
troops			
troop			
victory		victorious	victoriously
victor			

Definitions and Examples

1. **blow up** (a) {separable} [to explode]

    The car caught fire and burned when it **blew up**.
    They put a bomb in the building and **blew** it **up**.

    (b) {separable} [to inflate]

    The woman was very tired after she **blew up** 50 balloons for her
    daughter's party.

2. **victory** [the achievement of success in a battle or fight]

    Their **victory** over their enemy happened after ten years of fighting.
    The **victorious** army marched into the city.
    Our volleyball team was the **victor** at the end of the series of games.

3. **resist** [to fight against, with actions or words]

    Many citizens are **resisting** the government attempts to make them drive
    more slowly.
    The **resistance** fighters are hiding in the mountains; they attack the
    army whenever they can.
    I could not **resist** the idea of staying home from work today because the
    weather was so nice.

4. **arms** (a) [weapons]

    The occupation army has ordered the resistance fighters to lay down their
    arms and surrender.
    In many countries, ordinary citizens are not permitted to carry **arms**.

    (b) [assumed: the part of the body between the hand and the chest]

    He had a large box in his **arms**.

5. **outcome** [a result]

    We do not know what the **outcome** of the battle will be; it is not yet
    clear who is winning.
    There are two possible **outcomes** to this situation; the king will keep his
    position, or he will leave the country.

6. **give up** {separable} [to surrender or stop trying]

    Many of the enemy soldiers **gave up** and laid down their arms when they
    saw that they were losing the battle.
    My teacher told me not to **give up**; I can still pass if I study hard for the
    final exam.
    I had a dream of becoming a concert pianist, but I had to **give** it **up** when
    I injured my hand.

7. **tie up** {separable} (a) [to tie someone so that he cannot move]

> They found the soldier lying on the ground, **tied up**, but not hurt.
> They **tied** the clerk **up** during the robbery.

(b) [to keep busy]

> This new project will **tie** us **up** for months; we will not be able to work on anything else.
> My mother gets angry when I **tie up** the phone.
> The secretary said that the boss was **tied up** and could not come to the phone.

8. **flee** [to run away]

> The soldier lacked courage and **fled** from the battle.
> Many people have **fled** from the area of the fighting.

9. **hero** {feminine: heroine} (a) [a person who is admired for his or her achievements and positive characteristics]

> He is a **hero** because of his bravery during the war.
> Florence Nightingale was considered to be a **heroine** by the many soldiers whose lives she saved.

(b) [the main character in a piece of literature]

> The **hero** dies at the end of the book, but not before he tells the **heroine** that he loves her.

10. **enlist** (a) [to join the military]

> He **enlisted** in the navy when he graduated from high school.
> The army says that **enlistments** are increasing because unemployment is high.

(b) [to employ a person in the military]

> The army has **enlisted** 10,000 new men this year.

(c) [to get the support and help of]

> She **enlisted** her friends in her fight against the growth of crime in her neighborhood.

11. **campaign** [a period of competing or fighting to achieve some goal]

> The political **campaign** before American presidential elections lasts a long time.
> The government is having a **campaign** against smoking in public places.
> The navy's **campaign** to protect the northern beaches failed.

12. **junior** (a) [younger; less experienced; of lower rank]

   The **junior** officer in command of the soldiers had only been a lieutenant for one month before the battle.
   She joined the firm a year ago and is a **junior** partner now.

   (b) [2-19: a student in the year before the last year of high school or college]

   John stopped studying when he was a **junior** in college. He did not finish the last year.

13. **senior** (a) [older; more experienced; of higher rank]

   The **senior** officer present made the decision to surrender.
   The **senior** bank officials stated that they had no knowledge of their employee's crimes.

   (b) [2-19: a student in the last year of high school or college]

   Students graduate at the end of their **senior** year.

14. **major** (a) [the army rank immediately above captain]

   She was promoted from captain to **major** last month.
   Our senior officer is a **major**.

   (b) [2-16: big; important]

   A **major** forest fire kills a lot of animals.

   (c) [2-19: to study courses in college in the subject most important for the student's degree]

   I **majored** in Spanish in college and then got a job in Spain.

15. **conquer** [to be victorious over]

   Their superior weapons quickly helped them **conquer** their enemy.
   The **conquered** people still hated the enemy army in their country.

16. **die down** [to become quiet or calm]

   The fighting **died down** after three hours when the defenders of the town gave up.
   The president waited for the noise to **die down** before he began to speak.

17. **discipline** (a) [order gained by enforced obedience]

   He did not like the army because of the strict **discipline**.
   Parents must **discipline** their children.

   (b) [self control]

   It takes a lot of **discipline** to eat less and lose weight.

   (c) [a subject that is taught; a field of study]

   She has not yet decided which **discipline** to major in at college.

18. **give away** {separable} (a) [to reveal; to show the true situation]

> We had orders not to make any noise so that we would not **give** our position **away** to the enemy.
> He said that he was not afraid, but his shaking hands **gave** him **away**.

(b) [to give to someone]

> That rich man has **given away** a lot of money.

19. **lay in** [to collect and store (usually food or other supplies)]

> There is a storm predicted for tomorrow. We should **lay in** a supply of food and fuel to prepare for it.
> His job is to **lay in** supplies before the soldiers begin their long march through the desert.

20. **rebel** [a person who fights against an established government or situation]

> The **rebels** have blown up several government buildings.
> She is a **rebel** and disagrees with all the other scientists who are working on projects similar to hers.
> Children often act quite **rebelliously** toward their parents.
> At the end of the eighteenth century, the Americans **rebelled** against their English rulers.

21. **retreat** [to go in the opposite direction from a battle or some other dangerous situation]

> The major decided to **retreat** because his men did not have sufficient arms to fight with.
> Their **retreat** lasted for two hours.
> They **retreated** from the flood waters to the top of a hill.

22. **struggle** (against) (a) [to make strong, violent efforts against opposition]

> He **struggled** against his attacker.
> The **struggling** child tried to run away from his mother.

(b) [to fight against hardships]

> Their **struggle** to find food in the jungle took all of their time.

23. **troops** {usually plural} [soldiers]

> The major commanded 1,000 **troops**.
> We will have to retreat; the **troops** are too tired to advance.

24. **troop** [a group of people]

> The **troop** of soldiers retreated rapidly.
> The **troop** of tourists stopped to take pictures of the fountain.

Introductory Exercises

A. Match each word with its definition.

____	**1.** to join the military	**a.**	arms
____	**2.** a result	**b.**	blow up
____	**3.** the army rank immediately above captain	**c.**	campaign
		d.	conquer
____	**4.** a person who fights against an established government or situation	**e.**	die down
		f.	discipline
____	**5.** soldiers	**g.**	enlist
____	**6.** order gained by enforced obedience	**h.**	flee
		i.	give away
____	**7.** younger; less experienced; of lower rank	**j.**	give up
____	**8.** to surrender or stop trying	**k.**	hero
____	**9.** weapons	**l.**	junior
____	**10.** to keep someone or something very busy	**m.**	lay in
		n.	major
____	**11.** a man who is admired for his achievements and positive characteristics	**o.**	outcome
		p.	rebel
		q.	resist
____	**12.** older; more experienced; of higher rank	**r.**	retreat
____	**13.** to be victorious over	**s.**	senior
____	**14.** to reveal; to show the true situation	**t.**	struggle
____	**15.** to go in the opposite direction from a battle or some other dangerous situation	**u.**	tie up
		v.	troops
____	**16.** a group of people	**w.**	troop
____	**17.** to fight against, with actions or words	**x.**	victory
____	**18.** to run away		
____	**19.** a period of competing or fighting to achieve some goal		
____	**20.** the achievement of success in a battle or fight		
____	**21.** to become quiet or calm		
____	**22.** to collect and store (usually food or other supplies)		
____	**23.** to make strong, violent efforts against opposition		

B. Answer each question with a word from the word form chart.

1. What might you do if you know that you cannot win a fight? (three answers)
2. What do bombs do to buildings?
3. Who is someone who risks his life to save others?
4. What happens before an election?
5. What kind of officer is a general?
6. What kind of officer is a lieutenant?
7. What do soldiers use to fight?
8. What might people do if they don't like their government? (three answers)
9. What can you do to a prisoner to keep him from fleeing?
10. What does an army captain become when he is promoted?
11. What should you do about food and other supplies before a big snowstorm?
12. What should you do if you want to be in the military?
13. What are winning and losing examples of?
14. What is the successful outcome of a war?

Study Exercises

C. Write **T** if the sentence is true and **F** if it is false.

_____ 1. Parents like their children to be well disciplined.

_____ 2. Rebels resist the established government.

_____ 3. A campaign happens after the election.

_____ 4. Soldiers expecting a positive outcome often retreat from a battle.

_____ 5. A victory is a positive outcome.

_____ 6. Conquerors are usually weak.

_____ 7. Senior officers tell junior officers what to do.

_____ 8. The fighting dies down at the end of a battle.

_____ 9. Victorious troops usually flee.

_____ 10. People admire a heroine.

_____ 11. A person who is tied up may struggle.

_____ 12. Troops sometimes blow up bridges.

_____ 13. A person who is fleeing from enemy troops wants to give away his position to them.

D. Complete the analogies with a word from the word form chart.

1. gun : shoot :: bomb : _____
2. criminal : flee :: troops : _____
3. experiment : result :: war : _____
4. thought : control :: behavior : _____
5. players : team :: soldiers : _____
6. rebel : resistance :: conquerer : _____
7. club : join :: navy : _____
8. tell : secret :: _____ : position
9. sports : champion :: war : _____

E. Circle the phrase which does not fit.

1. tie up	**a.** the criminal **b.** the prisoner **c.** the machine **d.** the glass	6. fill in for	**a.** the baby **b.** your friend **c.** an employee **d.** the teacher
2. carry out	**a.** the university **b.** the order **c.** the assignment **d.** the experiment	7. lay in	**a.** provisions **b.** supplies **c.** friends **d.** food
3. give away	**a.** your position **b.** someone's secret **c.** someone's location **d.** someone's breath	8. get on with	**a.** the outcome **b.** the procedure **c.** the problem **d.** the work
4. do over	**a.** the report **b.** the death **c.** the job **d.** the assignment	9. look over	**a.** the situation **b.** the report **c.** the dark **d.** the journal
5. give up	**a.** the struggle **b.** the surrender **c.** the effort **d.** the idea		

F. In each blank, write the most appropriate word or phrase from the word form chart.

   The American War of Independence was considered to be a minor rebellion against British authority until the seriousness of the (1) _____ struggle against British rule became obvious. The British expected a quick (2) _____ against the rebels. They knew

that the rebel army had little training and lacked (3) _____ .
Although many of the British (4) _____ were professional
soldiers, the men who (5) _____ in the rebel army were farmers
and store clerks who might (6) _____ at the first sign of actual
fighting. In addition, the British army had access to all the
(7) _____ and provisions which they needed. The British officers
were certain that the Americans, who had not had time to
(8) _____ weapons or food before the declaration of war, would
not be able to continue their (9) _____ throughout a long
(10) _____ . They expected that the rebels' enthusiasm for their
cause would gradually (11) _____ when the reality of war was
evident and that the rebel army would be forced to (12) _____ .
Unfortunately for the British, they did not recognize the depth of the
Americans' belief in their struggle.

Follow-up

G. Dictation: Write the sentences that your teacher reads aloud.

1. _____
2. _____
3. _____
4. _____
5. _____

H. Answer the following questions.

1. Do policemen in your country carry arms? What kind?
2. What kinds of political campaigns are there in your country? What happens during a campaign?
3. How do parents discipline their children in your country?
4. Do many people in your country enlist voluntarily in the military? Why or why not?
5. Have you ever had to give up a dream for your future? Explain.
6. Who is the most respected hero in the history of your country?
7. If you knew that a big storm was coming tomorrow, what supplies would you lay in?
8. Who is the most senior member of your family? The most junior?
9. Do you normally see any troops on the streets of this city? Of your hometown? Why or why not?

10. What was the greatest victory in your country's history? Has your country ever conquered another country? Which ones?
11. Has your country ever been conquered? By whom?

I. Describe an action of resistance or a rebellion that you know about.

Crime (A)

Word Form Chart

NOUN	VERB	ADJECTIVE	ADVERB
accusation	accuse	accusing	accusingly
		accused	
annoyance	annoy	annoying	annoyingly
		annoyed	
	break into		
	check up on		
	clear up		
concealment	conceal	concealed	
confinement	confine	confining	
		confined	
desperation		desperate	desperately
escort	escort		
evidence		evident	evidently
	get away		
	get away with		
inquiry	inquire	inquiring	
involvement	involve	involved	
kidnapper	kidnap	kidnapped	
	look into		
property			
punishment	punish	punishing	
ransom	ransom	ransomed	
release	release	released	
rifle			
sentence	sentence		
suspect	suspect	suspicious	suspiciously
suspicion			
task			

NOUN	VERB	ADJECTIVE	ADVERB
threat	threaten	threatening	threateningly
trial	try		
wealth		wealthy	
witness	witness		

Definitions and Examples

1. **annoy** [to bother]

   The police told me to call them immediately if the man **annoyed** me again.
   Any noise while I am studying **annoys** me.
   The phone calls are not a major problem; they are only an **annoyance**.

2. **conceal** [to hide]

   The robber carried a **concealed** weapon: a small gun, hidden in his pocket.
   You should **conceal** your money carefully so that no one steals it.

3. **witness** [a person who sees a crime or some other event]

   The police questioned all the **witnesses** to the robbery.
   The **witnesses** to the accident said it was not my fault.
   If you **witness** a crime, you should call the police.

4. **confine** [to keep a person or animal in a prisonlike situation]

   After her arrest, she was **confined** for six months; then, they let her leave the jail.
   He should be **confined** so that he cannot hurt anyone else.
   Most people fear **confinement** in any small or dark place.

5. **evidence** [physical proof concerning a crime]

   The police searched the scene of the crime for **evidence**.
   The jury did not believe the **evidence** against her and decided she was innocent of the murder.

6. **kidnap** [to steal a person; to take and hold a person against his or her will]

   They **kidnapped** the small girl and demanded money from her parents.
   The **kidnappers** killed their victim when the police got too close to them.

7. **look into** [to investigate]

   The police promised to **look into** the robbery although there was very little evidence.
   My boss said that he would **look into** my complaint about the lack of safety rules in the factory.

8. **punish** [to do something negative to a person because he has done something wrong]

> The mother **punished** her little boy because he had lied to her.
> He was not allowed to watch television for a week.
> His **punishment** for his crime was five years of confinement in a state prison.

9. **ransom** [money paid to kidnappers in order to get a kidnap victim back]

> The kidnappers demanded $100,000 **ransom** for the return of the child.
> The government paid a high **ransom** for the return of the president.

10. **release** [to permit someone or something to leave some confinement]

> The kidnappers **released** the executive after the ransom had been paid.
> The police **released** the woman because there was not enough evidence against her.

11. **trial** (a) [the procedure in a court of law during which a person is judged guilty or innocent]

> His **trial** lasted for three weeks, but he was finally found to be innocent.
> The jury heard a lot of strong evidence during the five-day **trial**.
> She was **tried** and found guilty last year.

(b) [a source of annoyance]

> Their three-year-old child is quite a **trial**; she is always crying.

(c) [a test]

> This company has a two-month **trial** period for all new employees; after two months, the final decision about their continued employment is made.

12. **escort** [to go with another person in order to guard or accompany him or her]

> The police guard **escorted** the arrested criminal to jail.
> Her friend **escorted** her to the wedding.
> The president's **escorts** walked in front of him.

13. **accuse** [to state that a person is to blame for a crime or other negative action, especially to officially blame someone]

> The police **accused** her of murdering her boss.
> The **accused** man was taken to jail.
> The child **accused** his friend of lying to him.
> The police must prove their **accusations**.

14. **inquiry** [a systematic investigation, often of an event of public interest]

> The police **inquiry** into the death of Mr. Smith was not a success; they found no useful evidence.
> During the **inquiry**, it was discovered that her death had not been an accident.

15. **inquire** [to investigate; to ask]

> The police are **inquiring** about her movements on the night of the murder.

16. **rifle** [a type of gun which is several feet long]

> The soldiers carried their **rifles** on their shoulders.
> A high-powered **rifle** can shoot a long distance.

17. **sentence** [a judgment given in a court which specifies the punishment for the criminal]

> The judge read the **sentence**: "Twenty years in the state prison."
> The prisoner will be **sentenced** as soon as the trial is finished.

18. **task** (a) [an assigned piece of work, which must often be finished within a certain time period]

> The teacher gave each of us a different **task** to accomplish during the hour.
> The boss was pleased that his newest employee always finished her **tasks** quickly.

   (b) [something hard or unpleasant that has to be done]

> I have been laboring over this **task** for weeks.
> My least favorite **task** is cleaning the bathroom.

19. **threaten** [to express intent to injure or damage]

> The prisoner **threatened** to kill the judge who sentenced him to prison.
> The large dog made a **threatening** sound.
> That disease is a **threat** to the whole city.
> The escaped prisoner will be a **threat** until he is caught again.

20. **suspicion** [doubt that a person is innocent or honest]

> There is **suspicion** that she killed her husband.
> The police **suspect** that she poisoned him.
> She was acting **suspiciously** during the week before he died: she did not go home at all.

21. **wealth** [the money or possessions someone has]

> He lost his **wealth** through a bad business deal.
> **Wealthy** people often have large houses.

22. **property** (a) [the land owned by someone]

> She wants to build a small house on her **property**.
> People in this city have to pay **property** taxes.

   (b) [the things owned by someone]

> The police recovered the stolen **property** and returned it to the owner.

23. **break into** [to use force to enter a building without permission]

> The men **broke into** the bank and stole $50,000.
> He **broke into** our house and kidnapped my brother.

24. **check up on** [to investigate]

> The police will **check up on** all the witnesses' stories.
> My parents are so suspicious! They are always **checking up on** me.

25. **clear up** {separable} (a) [to find the solution]

> The police expect to **clear up** the mystery soon.
> This situation is complicated, but we can **clear** it **up** by reviewing last night's events.

>> (b) [5-3: to become clear]

>> This bad weather should **clear up** soon.

26. **desperate** [having little or no hope]

> The **desperate** bank robber shot one of the witnesses.
> The **desperate** parents prayed for the life of their dying child.

27. **involve** (a) [to bring into a situation]

> The murderer did not want his family to be **involved** with his trial.
> The police think that a large gang of criminals is **involved** in the robberies.

(b) [to include as a necessary part]

> Becoming a lawyer **involves** many years of studying.

28. **get away** [to escape]

> The prisoners **got away** during the night.
> My pet bird **got away** and never came back.

29. **get away with** [to escape punishment for]

> They **got away with** their crime because there was insufficient evidence against them.
> My mother always lets my little brother **get away with** everything.

Introductory Exercises

A. Match each word with its definition.

  _c_   **1.** to use force to enter a building without permission

  _v_   **2.** doubt that a person is innocent or honest

  _u_   **3.** a judgment given in a court which specifies the punishment for the criminal

  _a_   **4.** to state that a person is to blame for a crime

  _s_   **5.** to permit someone or something to leave some confinement

  _q_   **6.** to do something negative to a person because he has done something wrong

  _g_   **7.** to keep a person in a prisonlike situation

  _b_   **8.** to bother

  _f_   **9.** to hide

  _j_   **10.** physical proof concerning a crime

  _r_   **11.** the money paid to kidnappers in order to get a kidnap victim back

  _y_   **12.** the procedure in a court of law during which a person is judged guilty or innocent

  _l_   **13.** a systematic investigation

  _t_   **14.** a type of gun which is several feet long

  _n_   **15.** to steal a person

  _aa_   **16.** a person who sees a crime or some other event

  _i_   **17.** to go with another person in order to guard or accompany him or her

  _x_   **18.** to express intent to injure or damage

  _p_   **19.** the land owned by someone

  _h_   **20.** having little or no hope

  _k_   **21.** to escape

a. accuse
b. annoy
c. break into
d. check up on
e. clear up
f. conceal
g. confine
h. desperate
i. escort
j. evidence
k. get away
l. inquiry
m. involve
n. kidnap
o. look into
p. property
q. punish
r. ransom
s. release
t. rifle
u. sentence
v. suspicion
w. task
x. threaten
y. trial
z. wealth
aa. witness

B.   Answer each question with a word from the word form chart.

1. What do the police need to find to solve a mystery? *inquiry evidence*
2. Name a type of gun. *rifle*
3. Who travels with a president? *escort*
4. What do thieves do to wealthy peoples' houses? *punish break into*
5. What do parents pay for the release of a kidnapped child? *ransom*
6. What do criminals do with their weapons so that the police cannot see *conseal* them?
7. What do parents do to their children who behave badly? *punish*
8. How does a criminal feel when he sees no hope of escape? *desperate*
9. Name two two- or three-word verbs meaning "investigate." *check up on , inquire look into*
10. What are you if you see a crime? *witness*
11. During what procedure is a person judged guilty or innocent? *trial*
12. What is ten years in prison an example of? *confine sentence punishment*
13. When a ransom is paid to kidnappers, what should happen to the victim? *release*
14. What can you call the land you own? *property*
15. What is a job that you have to do? *task*
16. What is the statement, "I'm going to kill you," an example of? *threaten*
17. What does a loud noise do to you if you are trying to sleep? *annoy*
18. What do you call a person who the police think committed a crime? *suspect*

Study Exercises

C.   Write **T** if the sentence is true and **F** if it is false.

F   1. Most people enjoy receiving punishment.

T   2. If something is concealed, you cannot easily see it.

T   3. A cage is a place of confinement.

F   4. People kill people with rifles.

T   5. Witnesses give statements about evidence at trials.

F   6. A kidnapping victim must be a child.

F   7. If the police suspect someone of committing a crime, they may accuse that person.

T   8. The purpose of a police inquiry is to gather evidence concerning a crime.

F   9. Threats are always carried out.

T   10. People usually enjoy being released from confinement.

T   11. An annoying noise is one that bothers you.

F   12. Criminals want to receive harsh sentences.

F   13. Murderers get away with their crimes when they are found guilty at their trials.

D. Complete the analogies with a word or phrase from the word form chart.

1. friend : companion :: accompany : ___colleague___ *escort*

2. steal : jewel :: ___kidnap___ : person

3. disagree : argue :: ___*suspect*___ : accuse

4. white : black :: poverty : ___*wealthy*___

5. research : facts :: inquiry : ___evidence___

6. doctor : fee :: kidnapper : ___ransom___

7. promise : help :: hurt : ___threaten___

E. In each blank, write the most appropriate two- or three-word verb from the list below. You may use each verb more than once.

blow up	tie up	clear up
die down	lay in	get away with
give away	break into	look into
give up	check up on	

1. In order to ___~~break into~~ *blow up*___ the bank, the robbers used a bomb.

2. The robbers ___blow up___ the night guard, whom they found inside the bank.

3. The police decided to ___look into___ the information that the bank guard gave them about the robbers.

4. The police thought that they could ___check up on___ their uncertainty about the identities of the robbers by ___check up on___ any similar robberies in the past.

5. The robbers finally ___give up___ when the police cornered them in their hotel room.

F. In each blank, write the most appropriate word or phrase from the word form chart.

Kidnapping became a federal crime in the United States in 1932 after the kidnapping of Charles Lindbergh's baby son. The new law also stated that a kidnapper could be (1) ___punished___ to death.

The kidnapper of the Lindbergh baby (2) ___broke into___ the Lindbergh house and took the child from his second floor bedroom. A large sum of money was demanded for the (3) ___ransom___ of the child. The Lindberghs paid the (4) ___ransom___, but several days later the child was found, murdered.

The police (5) ___confined___ Bruno Hauptmann, a carpenter, of the kidnapping and murder on the basis of a variety of physical

(6) ___evidence___ found at the homes of both Lindbergh and Hauptmann

during the (7) _____ carried out by the New Jersey police.

Throughout his (8) _____ , Hauptmann insisted that he had not

been (9) _____ in the kidnapping. However, Hauptmann was

(10) _____ to die in the electric chair.

Follow-up

G. Dictation: Write the sentences that your teacher reads aloud.

1. _____
2. _____
3. _____
4. _____
5. _____

H. Answer the following questions.

1. Have you ever witnessed a crime? What happened?
2. Who is the wealthiest person in your country?
3. What is the typical sentence for a person found guilty of kidnapping in your country?
4. Which government officials in your country have official escorts when they travel?
5. What do you find most annoying when you are in a crowd?
6. How do parents in your country typically punish their children?
7. What kind of people tend to be kidnapped? Why?
8. Have you ever used a rifle? For what purpose?
9. Is a person who is accused of a crime always confined in your country? Explain.
10. Where is a good place to conceal your money in your home?
11. Do many criminals in your country get away with their crimes? Explain.
12. If you see someone outside your home at night, what kind of behavior do you consider to be suspicious?

I. Describe the court systems in your country. What are trials like?

Food

Word Form Chart

NOUN	VERB	ADJECTIVE	ADVERB
calorie			
capacity			
	chew up		
	cut down on		
	cut out		
diet	diet	dietary	
dinner	dine	dining	
diner			
essential		essential	essentially
fill up	fill up		
garbage			
ingredient			
	live on		
mix	mix	mixed, mixing	
mixture			
nutrient			
nutrition		nutritional	nutritionally
nutritiousness		nutritious	nutritiously
oil	oil	oily	
		oiled	
pan			
plastic		plastic	
portion	portion out		
produce			
	put away		
quantity	quantify	quantitative	quantitatively
recipe			
	run out of		
snack	snack		

NOUN	VERB	ADJECTIVE	ADVERB
starvation	starve	starving starved	
supper			

Definitions and Examples

1. **supper** [the evening meal, frequently the main meal of the day]

   We had a lot to eat for **supper**.
   My brother missed **supper** because he came home late.

2. **diet** (a) [a reduction in the amount or kinds of food eaten in order to lose weight or to stay healthy]

   I went on a **diet** to lose the weight I had gained over the holidays.

   (b) [what you eat from day to day]

   A proper **diet** and enough exercise will help keep you healthy.

3. **quantity** [an amount]

   The **quantity** of food you eat has an effect on how much you weigh.
   Even though he eats small **quantities** of food, he gains weight because the food is very fattening.

4. **produce** (a) [fresh fruits and vegetables]

   We buy much more **produce** than meat when we go shopping.
   Farmers frequently sell their **produce** at the roadside.

   (b) [2-2: to make]

   Italy **produces** shoes.

5. **dine** [to eat any meal, but generally dinner]

   The Maxwells **dined** at the new French restaurant downtown.
   We usually **dine** at 6:00 P.M.

6. **diner** (a) [a person who dines]

   The **diners** had a delicious meal and a wonderful time at the dinner dance.

   (b) [a restaurant that looks like a railroad car]

   Diners are usually much less formal and less expensive than other restaurants.

7. **essential** [basic; necessary]

   Food, sleep, and housing are **essential** human needs.
   He is **essentially** a careful person, but sometimes he makes silly mistakes.

8. **cut down (on)** [to reduce the quantity (of)]

> Marge **cut down on** how much bread she ate in order to lose weight.
> In order to protect your heart, you must **cut down on** the amount of salt and fat you eat.
> I eat too much; I should **cut down**.

9. **cut out** {separable} [to completely stop using or doing something]

> My dad **cut out** smoking and drinking on his doctor's orders.
> We **cut** sugar **out** of our daily diet.

10. **portion** [the quantity of food usually served to one person; a part of a whole]

> I am not very hungry, so give me only a small **portion** of meat and only a spoonful of potatoes.

11. **portion out** {separable} [to divide into portions and distribute]

> The boss **portioned out** the work so that no one would have to do the entire job; each person would have a small task.

12. **starve** [to suffer from extreme hunger; to die from hunger]

> It is possible to diet so strictly that you essentially **starve** yourself.
> Many people in Africa have died from **starvation** because of the lack of rain.

13. **garbage** (a) [useless food items that you throw away]

> You must be sure to take the **garbage** out so that the kitchen does not smell.

> (b) [anything useless]

> > A: Why do you collect such **garbage**?
> > B: You might think these are **garbage**, but I enjoy old magazines and photographs!

14. **fill up on** [to satisfy your hunger; to make yourself full]

> We **filled up on** meat and potatoes.
> There was not much meat, so we **filled up on** rice.

15. **fill up (with)** {separable} [to make something full]

> He **filled** his plate **up** with vegetables.
> The psychology course was so popular that it quickly **filled up**.

16. **live on** [to exist with the help of something; to eat primarily one thing]

> A well-known expression in English is "Man cannot **live on** bread alone."
> We were so poor that year that we had to **live on** potatoes and bread.
> Students in the United States sometimes **live on** hamburgers.

17. **mix** [to combine, often so that the separate parts are no longer obvious]

> She **mixed** the onions, pepper, salt, and beef together. Then she put the
> **mixture** in the oven.
> Chemists **mix** many chemicals when doing experiments.
> It is easy to make good cakes if you buy a cake **mix** from the store.

18. **ingredient** [something added or required, often to form a mixture]

> Flour, eggs, salt, butter, and sugar are some of the **ingredients** necessary
> for a cake.
>
> A: What are the **ingredients** of a happy family?
> B: Love, trust, and communication are essential for a happy home.

19. **capacity (for)** (a) [volume; the ability to hold something]

> The room has a sixty-person **capacity**.
> The **capacity** of this bottle is one liter.

(b) [the ability to learn; an ability]

> Barb has a natural **capacity** for chemistry.

(c) [the maximum amount of production; as much as possible]

> A: What is the **capacity** of that automobile plant?
> B: It can produce over 1,000 cars each day.
>
> The factory was operating below **capacity**.
> There was a **capacity** crowd at the concert.

(d) [the position in which one works or serves]

> He works in the **capacity** of assistant manager.

20. **run out (of)** [to have no more of something]

> We **ran out of** food before the party ended.
> It seems that our money always **runs out** before the end of the month.

21. **recipe** [the instructions for preparing a type of food]

> My mother cooks so well that she never has to follow **recipes**.
> The **recipe** had only three main steps.

22. **nutritious** [having or providing the ingredients necessary for good health;
    healthful]

> Meat, vegetables, and milk are all very **nutritious**; they all provide the
> body with the energy it needs.
> It is important to pay attention to **nutrition**; you should be careful to eat
> all the food items your body needs.
> In order to stay healthy, we must eat foods which contain essential
> **nutrients**.

23. **put away** {separable} [to put something back in the place that it belongs; to remove something from sight]

> Margarita **put** the dishes **away** when they were dry.
> The children **put away** their clean clothes; they hung their shirts in the closet.
> When the teacher told them to **put** all their books **away**, they put them in their desks.

24. **pan** [a shallow, wide, open container used for holding liquids, for cooking, etc.]

> She cooked the eggs in a **pan** on top of the stove.
> They cooked the fish in a **pan** in the oven.

25. **plastic** [a material that can be shaped or molded]

> Containers that used to be made of glass are now usually made of **plastic**.
> **Plastic** can be clear or it can be colored.
> She covered the leftover meat with **plastic** wrap.

26. **oil** [a liquid made from animal, vegetable, or mineral materials and used for fuel, food, cooking, etc.]

> We cooked the eggs in a little bit of corn **oil**.
> People frequently put vegetable **oil** on their salads.
> **Oil** will float on water.

27. **chew up** {separable} [to break up food, etc., completely with your teeth]

> The child **chewed** his food **up** carefully.
> The dog **chewed up** my shoes; they are ruined!

28. **calorie** [a unit of energy; the amount of heat required to raise the temperature of one kilogram of water by one degree Centigrade]

> Americans are often worried about how many **calories** there are in the food they eat.
> Different types of exercise will burn off different amounts of **calories**.
> Water has no **calories**, while oil has many.

29. **snack** [a small quantity of food eaten between meals to satisfy hunger until mealtime]

> Fruit or a piece of cake and a glass of milk are frequently eaten as **snacks**.
> **Snacking** can cause you to lose your appetite at mealtime.

Introductory Exercises

A.   Match each word with its definition.

____ **1.** a combination of ingredients	**a.** calorie
____ **2.** an amount	**b.** capacity
____ **3.** a liquid used in cooking	**c.** cut down on
____ **4.** good for your health	**d.** cut out
____ **5.** to have no more of something	**e.** diet
____ **6.** severe hunger	**f.** diner
____ **7.** the main meal of the day	**g.** essential
____ **8.** a shallow container	**h.** fill up on
____ **9.** to reduce the amount	**i.** garbage
____ **10.** to exist with the help of something	**j.** live on
____ **11.** an ability	**k.** mixture
____ **12.** fresh fruits and vegetables	**l.** nutritious
____ **13.** your share of food	**m.** oil
____ **14.** basic; necessary	**n.** pan
____ **15.** a unit of energy	**o.** plastic
____ **16.** not to use anymore	**p.** portion
____ **17.** anything you throw away	**q.** produce
____ **18.** a place where you can eat	**r.** quantity
____ **19.** a small quantity of food eaten between meals to satisfy hunger until mealtime	**s.** run out of
	t. snack
____ **20.** to make yourself full with something	**u.** starvation
	v. supper

B.   Complete each sentence with a word or words from the word form chart.

1. To cook something you can follow the directions in a

   _____ .

2. If you are getting fat, you should go on a _____ .

3. Three meals are breakfast, lunch, and _____ .

4. Food with a lot of oil and sugar has a lot of _____ .

5. If you don't eat anything for two months, you will _____ .

6. You can cook food in a _____ .

7. When something is very important, it is _____ .

8. If you buy fruits and vegetables, you are buying _____ .

9. When you combine flour, sugar, and oil, you have made a

    _____ .

10. Food that is good for you is _____ .

11. When you clean the house, you should _____ things

    _____ .

12. If you are getting fat, you should _____ how much you eat

    and _____ certain food completely.

Study Exercises

C. Write **T** if the sentence is true and **F** if it is false.

_____ **1.** People drink oil with their supper.

_____ **2.** If you fill up on food, you will starve.

_____ **3.** Recipes can help you cook.

_____ **4.** "Dine" means the same as "eat."

_____ **5.** Garbage is good for dessert.

_____ **6.** Nutritious food is necessary for a good diet.

_____ **7.** A recipe might tell you to mix several ingredients together.

_____ **8.** Produce comes from animals.

_____ **9.** If you want to lose weight, you should cut down oil and high-calorie foods.

_____ **10.** Starving is a healthy way to lose weight.

_____ **11.** If a cake is cut into ten pieces, there are ten portions.

_____ **12.** People make shopping lists of the things that they have run out of.

_____ **13.** Large quantities of coffee are necessary for a good diet.

_____ **14.** You cut out vegetables and meat if you want to make vegetable soup.

_____ **15.** Chewing up your food will reduce calories.

_____ **16.** Snacking too much is a frequent cause of weight gain.

D.   There are seven errors in the following recipe. Circle the errors.

Vegetable Soup

Ingredients:

½ pound beef	4 plastic tomatoes
4 medium potatoes	fresh corn
4 large carrots	fresh green beans
10 calories	salt and pepper
1 large onion	

Wash and clean all vegetables. Cut down the meat into small pieces. Add meat to a pot half filled up on water. Begin to cook meat. While waiting for meat to cook, cut out the remaining vegetables. Add salt and pepper and all vegetables except potatoes. Cook until carrots are half cooked, and then put the potatoes away in the pot. Continue to cook until all vegetables are starving. Add more salt or pepper if necessary.

E.   Read the passage and answer the questions that follow.

Dieting to lose weight has become very popular in recent years. People have become more health conscious and try to take better care of their bodies by eating more nutritiously and exercising more regularly to lose any unnecessary fat that they

5 may have. In the United States these days, there are not as many people filling up between meals on "garbage foods" such as potato chips or chocolate candy. Instead, they have either cut that snack out completely, or they choose a more nutritious snack such as an apple or a small salad. They also cut down on the quantity of

10 certain foods that they eat at each meal. For example, they will have a smaller portion than usual of beef, a food which is high in fat content and calories, and eat larger portions of vegetables, which are lower in fat and calories, yet very high in certain nutrients.

15   Not only are people being careful about what they eat, but they are also concerned with how they eat and how their meals are prepared. People are taking more time for each meal. Many avoid eating hamburgers at fast-food restaurants and choose to eat a salad or a sandwich of more healthful ingredients in a quiet

20 restaurant with a more leisurely atmosphere. There they can dine without the pressure of having to leave because someone else is waiting for their table. At home, they also try to take enough time to eat a relaxed dinner without phone or TV interruptions. To ensure a more nutritious meal, many Americans have become

25 "recipe-conscious"; that is, they are cooking with recipes that call for fewer fattening ingredients, such as oil, butter, sugar, and certain types of meats. If butter is an essential ingredient, however, they might choose to substitute vegetable oil, which is lower in fat and calories.

30   While dieting may be viewed as beneficial, it has also become

a serious problem for Americans, particularly for young women who are worried about being thin like the models in fashion magazines. Some young women in the United States today are dieting to the point of illness, an illness which is called

35 "anorexia." Dieting for them has actually become a psychological addiction. They eat so little that they can lose as much as fifty percent of their total body weight, and although they are very thin, they still insist that they are fat. They are so concerned with counting calories and with cutting down on the types and

40 quantities of food they eat, that they are essentially starving themselves. There have actually been cases of young women dieting to the point of starving themselves to death. The current wave of exercising, dieting, and problems produced as a result of exercising and dieting has caused many organizations to begin

45 educating the public. Many schools, hospitals, health organizations, newspapers, and magazines, for example, are offering classes and printing booklets and articles, to inform the public of the proper way to exercise and diet, of the dangers of dieting too rapidly, and of the places people can go for medical help if they

50 find themselves on the road to "diet addiction."

1. Why are people dieting more these days? _____

_____

2. What are some changes that they have made in the types and quantities of food they eat? _____

_____

3. What changes have people made in the atmosphere of mealtime? _____

_____

4. What changes have they made in how they prepare meals? _____

_____

5. What serious problem can overdieting cause? _____

_____

6. What happens to a person who develops this dieting addiction? _____

_____

7. How are organizations trying to help people with dieting addictions? _____

_____

Follow-up

F.   Dictation: Write the sentences that your teacher reads aloud.

1. _____
2. _____
3. _____
4. _____
5. _____

G.   Answer the following questions.

1. What are some foods typical of the diet in your country?
2. What are some typical snack foods?
3. What foods would you cut out or cut down on if you wanted to lose weight?
4. What type of diet plan would you suggest for the person who wants to lose weight carefully?
5. What is your opinion on dieting to lose weight?
6. What are the ingredients in your favorite dish? What is the basic recipe for this dish; that is, how do you make it?
7. What are some ways in which governments or organizations or individual people can help families who are near starvation?

H.   Describe the typical dinner in your country, region, or family. Include information on the time you eat, how long the meal lasts, what you have, etc.

Science/Research

Word Form Chart

NOUN	VERB	ADJECTIVE	ADVERB
analysis	analyze	analytic	analytically
analyst		analytical	
analyzer			
area			
battery			
carbon	carbonize		
conduct	conduct	conductible	
conductor			
conduction			
conductibility			
	contract	contracted	
contraction		contractible	
current			
emission	emit	emissive	
emitter			
emissary			
formula	formulate		
formulation			
	hit on		
hypothesis	hypothesize	hypothetical	hypothetically
		invisible	invisibly
nucleus		nuclear	
particle		particular	particularly
particulate			
radiation	radiate	radiated	
radiator		radiating	
radiance		radiant	
ray			
statistics		statistical	statistically
statistic			

NOUN	VERB	ADJECTIVE	ADVERB
statistician			
table			
	think through		
	think up		
tryout	try out		
	turn up		
variety	vary	varying	variably
variation		variable	
variant		varied	
		various	variously
workout	work out		

Definitions and Examples

1. **analyze** [to examine the parts in order to determine the essential characteristics]

    The data from this experiment will be difficult to **analyze**.
    What is Professor Marsden's **analysis** of the language in this poem?

2. **work out** (a) {separable} [to solve]

    Let's **work** this problem **out** together.
    We have **worked out** such problems before.

    (b) [to add up to]

    The total **works out** to 487.
    The payments **work out** to $100 a month.

    (c) [5-7: to result in success]

    The new project has **worked out** well.

3. **vary** [to make different; to become different; to change]

    In this experiment, the scientist will **vary** the speed of the rocket.
    For good nutrition, you should eat a **variety** of foods.
    The weather here is **variable** in the spring.

4. **area** (a) [the measure or amount of a surface]

    You must know the length and width before you can calculate the **area**.
    The **area** of my room is 110 square feet.

    (b) [a field of study]

    Language and literature are related **areas** of study.
    What **area** of mathematics are you having difficulty with?

    (c) [2-3: a part of a city; a neighborhood; a space]

    The university students all live in the **area** near the campus.

5. **conduct** (a) [to lead; to direct; to manage]

Matthew had always wanted to **conduct** a famous orchestra.
My company **conducts** tours of historical buildings.

(b) [to serve as a medium or channel for heat, electricity, sound, etc.]

Silver **conducts** electricity very well.
Metals are usually efficient heat **conductors**.

(c) [personal behavior; a way of acting]

Martha's **conduct** in school improved after the teacher talked to her
    parents.
Judge Bracken **conducts** himself very professionally.

6. **battery** (a) [a small device which produces electricity]

Some toy trains work by **battery**.
My car will not start. I think it needs a new **battery**.

(b) [a group or series of similar or related things]

The school children were given a **battery** of tests.
The warship carried a large **battery** of guns.

7. **current** (a) [a flow or movement of water, air, electricity, etc.]

An electric **current** flows through these wires.
Strong water **currents** can be dangerous to swimmers.

(b) [**2-17**: new; present; popular; most recent]

Because of improvements in international media, **current** news
    is available almost everywhere.

8. **contract** (a) [to make shorter or smaller; to shrink]

Many things **contract** when they get colder.
"Isn't" is a **contraction** for "is not."

(b) [to get or acquire]

Children **contract** diseases more easily than adults.
Angela **contracted** several bad habits at summer camp.

(c) [**1-14**: a written agreement between two people]

My brother has signed a **contract** in which he agrees to buy a
    farm.

9. **carbon** [a substance which has the chemical symbol C. It occurs in the pure
state as the diamond.]

Carbon monoxide is a poisonous gas.
Fuel oil contains **carbon**.

10. **formula** {plural: formulae, formulas} (a) [a rule expressed in symbols]

Use this **formula** to determine the volume of a box: $V = L \times W \times H$.
When Jack studied physics he had to learn a lot of **formulae**.

(b) [a fixed or standard way of doing something; a set form]

All of her poetry seemed to be written according to the same **formula**.
There is no perfect **formula** for raising children.

(c) [a statement of the parts of a substance, in chemistry]

The chemical **formula** for carbon dioxide is CO_2.

11. **emit** [to release or send out]

How much light does this candle **emit**?
The machine **emits** clouds of gray smoke.
An **emissary** is a person who is sent as an agent.

12. **hit on** [to find, especially by accident; to guess correctly]

After only one try, we **hit on** the correct solution.
What luck it was to **hit on** such a great discovery.

13. **particle** [a very small piece or amount]

A **particle** of dust is almost invisible.
A **particle** of dirt in the eye is painful.

14. **nucleus** {plural: nuclei} (a) [the central part]

Four professional actors formed the **nucleus** of our theater group.

(b) [the central part of an atom]

Is **nuclear** war avoidable? Is **nuclear** energy safe?

15. **invisible** [not able to be seen; hidden from the eye]

Sound waves are usually **invisible**.
Children sometimes invent an **invisible** friend.

16. **hypothesis** {plural: hypotheses} [an assumption or a guess; a probable explanation]

What **hypothesis** can you think of to explain these events?
This is a **hypothetical** situation for the purpose of discussion.

17. **ray** [a line of light or other energy]

Rays of bright sunlight came through the rain clouds.
X-rays are useful medical tools.

18. **radiate** [to emit from the center in rays]

We can feel the heat **radiate** from the fire.
Nuclear **radiation** can cause sickness.

19. **turn up** {separable} [to fold up in order to make shorter]

> If your skirt is too long, you can always **turn** it **up**.

(b) [to make something louder or stronger]

> I cannot hear the radio. Please **turn** it **up**.
>
> **We turned up** the heat to make the room warmer.

(c) [to appear]

> The missing boy **turned up** at his friend's house.
> Three lost pens **turned up** when I finally cleaned my apartment.

20. **statistics** [numerical facts; the science of collecting numerical facts to show their significance]

> Our **statistics** show that the population is increasing.
> A **statistical** analysis of data requires knowledge of mathematics.

21. **try out** {separable} [to test]

> Can I **try out** this car before I buy it?
> If you have never cooked this dish before, you should **try** it **out** before you invite guests.

22. **table** (a) [a short list or other arrangement of information]

> A data **table** for this experiment is available in the physics lab.
> I use the **table** of contents to see what is included in a book.

> (b) [assumed: a piece of furniture having legs and a smooth flat top]

> The maid set the **table** for dinner.

23. **think through** {separable} [to think about something until an understanding or conclusion is reached]

> Please do not give me your answer until you've had time to **think** it **through**.
> If you **think through** the problem, you may discover a solution.

24. **think up** {separable} [to plan or discover by thinking; to invent (an idea or plan)]

> A: Did you **think up** the plan for this building by yourself?
> B: Yes. I **thought** it **up** without any help.

Introductory Exercises

A.   Match each word with its definition.

_____ **1.** to lead or manage	**a.** analyze
_____ **2.** not able to be seen	**b.** area
_____ **3.** to plan by thinking	**c.** battery
_____ **4.** a very small piece	**d.** carbon
_____ **5.** numerical facts	**e.** conduct
_____ **6.** to solve	**f.** contract
_____ **7.** a rule expressed in symbols	**g.** current
_____ **8.** a list of information	**h.** emit
_____ **9.** to find by accident	**i.** formula
_____ **10.** to make shorter or smaller	**j.** hit on
_____ **11.** a probable explanation	**k.** hypothesis
_____ **12.** to appear	**l.** invisible
_____ **13.** a line of light or other energy	**m.** nucleus
_____ **14.** the central part	**n.** particle
_____ **15.** a flow of electricity	**o.** radiate
_____ **16.** to send out	**p.** ray
_____ **17.** to test	**q.** statistics
_____ **18.** the substance with the chemical symbol C.	**r.** table
	s. think through
	t. think up
	u. try out
	v. turn up
	w. vary
	x. work out

B.   Answer each question with a word from the word form chart.

1. Who analyzes numerical facts?
2. What substance is present in a diamond?
3. What do we call the center of an atom?
4. What do you need to run a portable radio?
5. What happens to metal when it cools?
6. What do we call a tiny piece of dirt?
7. What has happened when we have found something by accident?
8. How can we make "cannot," "do not," and "is not" shorter?
9. What does wire do for electricity?
10. What do you learn when you multiply the length of a square times its width?
11. What can you do to a radio that is not loud enough?
12. What do we call weather that changes every day?
13. What should you do if you have a problem and you need to find a solution?

Study Exercises

C. Write **T** if the sentence is true and **F** if it is false.

_____ 1. A college campus is an area of study.

_____ 2. Batteries produce electric current.

_____ 3. There is a wide variety of books in a library.

_____ 4. Metal is a good electrical conductor.

_____ 5. Light travels in rays.

_____ 6. A hypothesis has not been proven.

_____ 7. The table of contents is a useful part of a book.

_____ 8. There is only one formula for a happy marriage.

_____ 9. Both light and heat radiate from the sun.

_____ 10. An experiment can sometimes prove that a hypothesis is correct.

_____ 11. The price of fresh fruit varies with the season.

_____ 12. If the radio is too loud, you should turn it up.

_____ 13. A scientist must sometimes think through a difficult problem.

_____ 14. Automobile emissions can be poisonous.

_____ 15. Statistics are used to analyze numerical facts.

D. Circle the word which does not fit.

1. emit	smoke heat snow light	6. turn up the	sound heat radio area
2. battery-powered	radio vehicle toy tree	7. invisible	movies forces rays gases
3. calculate the area of a	baby floor rug square	8. electric	current water ray air
4. analyze the	data invisible result statistics	9. conduct	philosophy an orchestra electricity a tour
5. nuclear	weapons jury reaction radiation	10. a variation in	temperature speed weight water

E.   Complete the analogies with a word or phrase from the word form chart.

1. expand : heat :: _____ : cold

2. fuel : car :: _____ : toy

3. guide : tourists :: _____ : orchestra

4. calculate : answer :: _____ : solution

5. invent : tool :: _____ : story

6. detective : clues :: _____ : numbers

7. length : line :: _____ : square

F.   Read the passage and answer the questions that follow.

> Our sun is just an ordinary star, not special in any way. But to
> the people on earth it is the source of life. The nuclear reactions
> that go on in the inner areas of the sun produce large quantities of
> energy. This energy is emitted in all directions in the form of light
> 5 and heat radiation. Only a small part of the radiated energy is used
> by our planet, Earth, for warmth and the development of life
> forms. Green plants have the ability to use some of the sun's
> visible radiation to produce food.
> The radiant energy emitted by our sun is not constant but
> 10 varies slightly in predictable cycles. Astronomers have long known
> about sunspots, which are major disturbances of the sun's outer
> regions. Statistical analysis of data concerning sunspot activity
> indicates a fairly well-defined frequency of occurrence. A full
> theoretical understanding of sunspot activity is not currently
> 15 available, but scientists hypothesize about the nature of the
> instabilities of the sun's atmosphere.
> Stars are more than lights in a dark night. They are varied and
> complex factories of our world. Carbon, which in one form is a
> diamond, is an essential substance contained in all living things.
> 20 The carbon in our bodies and in our oil was manufactured by
> the sun.

1. What kinds of energy are emitted by the sun? _____

_____

2. How do green plants use the sun's energy? _____

_____

3. Is the sun's emission of energy constant? _____

_____

4. What are sunspots? _____

_____

5. What have scientists learned from a statistical analysis of sunspot data?

_____

_____

6. Where can we find carbon? _____

_____

Follow-up

G. Dictation: Write the sentences that your teacher reads aloud.

1. _____
2. _____
3. _____
4. _____
5. _____

H. Answer the following questions.

1. What is a good heat conductor?
2. Name some things that require batteries.
3. Who might need to use statistics?
4. Name some things that are done by formula.
5. What would you like to try out before you buy it?
6. Do you live with an extended family or a nuclear family?
7. Can you guess the area of this page?
8. Name some things that are invisible.
9. What are the dangers of automobile and factory emissions?
10. Where can you find a wide variety of books, fruits, shoes, soap, etc.?

I. Explain the advantages and disadvantages of nuclear energy.

Entertainment

Word Form Chart

NOUN	VERB	ADJECTIVE	ADVERB
association	associate	associated	
brilliance		brilliant	
brush	brush		
	call off		
decency		decent	decently
indecency		indecent	indecently
	die away		
episode		episodic	episodically
frame	frame		
gallery			
	look forward to		
	make up		
opportunity		opportune	
passion		passionate	passionately
		portable	
rage	enrage	enraged	
		raging	
rehearsal	rehearse		
ridiculousness	ridicule	ridiculous	ridiculously
role			
romance			
romantic		romantic	romantically
shock	shock	shocking	shockingly
		shocked	
	spring up		
	(sprang, sprung)		
symmetry		symmetric	symmetrically
		symmetrical	
asymmetry		asymmetric	asymmetrically
		asymmetrical	

NOUN	VERB	ADJECTIVE	ADVERB
tear	tear (tore, torn)		
	tear up		
tragedy		tragic	tragically
versatility		versatile	

Definitions and Examples

1. **rehearsal** [a practice for a performance]

   They have **rehearsals** for the play every day now; the first performance is next week.

   You should **rehearse** your speech carefully so that you can present it well.

2. **opportunity** [a chance]

   He loved music, but because his family was poor, he had no **opportunity** to take lessons.

   That job sounds like an excellent **opportunity** for you; the pay is good and you will learn a lot.

   You should be careful of him. I think he is an **opportunist**; he only wants to be friends because he likes your swimming pool.

3. **die away** [to gradually get lower and disappear (said of noise)]

   His voice **died away** as the song ended.

   The loud noise of the jet **died away** when the pilot shut off the engines.

4. **gallery** (a) [a room or building for the showing of art]

   The art **gallery** was so crowded today that I could hardly see the paintings.

   The **gallery** was a long, thin room, with paintings hung on both walls.

   (b) [the highest area of a theater, which usually has the cheapest seats]

   We sat in the **gallery** at the concert because we could not afford better seats.

   (c) [the people watching a tennis or golf match]

   The golfer was angry because the **gallery** was making noise while he was making his shot.

5. **call off** {separable} [to cancel]

   The performance was **called off** because the singer was sick.

   They **called** the game **off** when it began to rain heavily.

6. **tear** [to separate parts of something by force]

   She stepped on the bottom of her dress and **tore** it.

   Be careful! This cloth will **tear** easily.

7. **tear up** {separable} [to tear into many parts by force]

> He **tore up** the notice and threw it away.
> If you make a mistake on a check, **tear** it **up**.

8. **association** [an organization of people with a common interest]

> The City Art **Association** is having a special show at the museum art gallery this month.
> We would like to form an **association** to promote dance programs for young people.

9. **associate** (a) [to join or connect together]

> People usually **associate** Alaska with very cold weather, but sometimes it is warm there in the summer.

> (b) [to be a companion with]

> You should not **associate** with criminals, or people will begin to think that you are a criminal too.

10. **enrage** [to make someone very angry]

> The destruction of the museum property so **enraged** the director that he was speechless.
> The **enraged** man hit the policeman and ran away.
> When she gets into a **rage**, it takes hours for her to calm down.

11. **role** [a character assigned or played (usually in a drama)]

> A famous actor played the **role** of the detective in the movie.
> The actors have been rehearsing their **roles** all week.

12. **portable** [able to be carried]

> We bought a small **portable** TV, which we can use in the kitchen and the bedroom.
> Many young people take **portable** radios to the beach with them.

13. **episode** (a) [one of a series of slightly connected stories or scenes]

> Let's not watch this program tonight; I have already seen this **episode** twice.

> (b) [an incident]

> I will never forget that **episode** with the police; I thought their questions to us would never end.

14. **brush** (a) [a tool used for painting or cleaning]

   > The artist used a thin **brush** to paint details on the picture.
   > I **brushed** the dust off my jacket.

   (b) [a light touch in passing]

   > The woman **brushed** my shoulder as she left the room.

   (c) [low vegetation (especially that which grows in a dry area)]

   > There were no real trees in sight, only **brush** covering the ground around us.

15. **tragedy** (a) [a very sad or unlucky event]

   > The death of their young son was a **tragedy**.
   > She started to cry when she heard the **tragic** news of the plane crash.

   (b) [a serious drama with a sad conclusion]

   > The newest play in town is a **tragedy** about a family's struggle against poverty.

16. **symmetrical** [balanced; able to be divided into two equal halves]

   > That picture is very **symmetrical**; the tree on the left is the same as the one on the right.
   > If you put that large piece of furniture there, it will ruin the **symmetry** of the room.
   > Her fashion designs are characterized by **asymmetry**; for example, sometimes the left half is white while the right side is black.

17. **passion** (a) [a very strong feeling, often love]

   > He felt such **passion** for her that he could not stop looking at her.

   (b) [an object of deep interest]

   > Her **passion** is reading history books.

18. **passionate** [emotional]

   > You should try to be less **passionate** and more logical if you want to succeed in the project.

19. **ridiculous** [laughable; foolish]

   > When he confessed his love for her, she laughed at him and he felt **ridiculous**.
   > Do not tell me that your dog ate your homework; that is a **ridiculous** excuse!
   > Children sometimes **ridicule** others who are different.

20. **shocking** [surprising or disgusting]

> The end of that movie was very **shocking**; I had not guessed that all the characters would be killed.
> We were **shocked** by the horrible scene after the explosion of the bomb.

21. **shock** (a) [a sudden change in the balance of a system]

> The sudden growth of imports caused a **shock** to the whole economy.
> Many of the victims of the accident were in **shock** when we arrived at the scene.

(b) [a sudden flow of electricity that affects a person]

> If you touch the radio when your hands are wet, you may get a bad **shock**.

22. **romantic** (a) [characterized by passionate love]

> Her boyfriend is so **romantic**; he always buys her flowers and prepares candlelight dinners for her.
> He is sad because his most recent **romance** ended badly; the woman ran away with another man.

(b) [an emotional attraction belonging to an especially heroic adventure or time period]

> Many people think that it would be **romantic** to be able to go back in time and live in another less modern period.

23. **brilliant** (a) [very shiny]

> Her diamond ring was **brilliant** in the sunlight.
> The waves shown **brilliantly** under the sun.

(b) [very clever or intelligent]

> That scientist's work has been **brilliant**; in only a few years, he has published a variety of important results.
> She writes **brilliantly**; her first three novels have been very successful.

24. **decent** (a) [appropriate according to public moral standards]

> This movie is not **decent** for children to see; it contains too much violence and too many passionate love scenes.
> That dress is so tight that it is **indecent**.

(b) [appropriate according to current standards of living]

> Everyone deserves to have **decent** housing and food to eat.
> I want to find a job that pays a **decent** salary.

25. frame (a) [an open structure made for supporting something]

The picture **frame** was made of dark wood.
The window **frames** need to be painted.
John has a wood **frame** house.
The **frames** of her glasses were bent in the accident,
     but the glass was not broken.

(b) [to produce false evidence against an innocent person
   so that he will be found guilty]

He was sentenced to twenty years in prison, but he says that he was
     framed by the person who had really committed the robbery.

26. look forward to [to anticipate with pleasure]

We are **looking forward to** seeing that new play; it is said to be very good.
He is **looking forward to** graduating from college and beginning work.

27. make up {separable} [to invent; to produce]

Children **make up** a lot of games when they play.
I enjoyed that novel until I reached the last part; the author should have
     made up a better conclusion.
That story he told was not true; he **made** it **up**.

28. spring up [to suddenly come to exist]

In 1950 there were almost no fast food restaurants in the United States;
     then they began to **spring up** all over the country.
When the weather turns warm in the spring, flowers begin to **spring up** in
     the parks.
Opposition to the current government is **springing up** all over the
     country.

29. versatile [having many uses or applications; capable of doing many things]

She is a very **versatile** actress; recently she has played an old woman and
     a young girl.
The **versatility** of this tool makes it a good investment; you can use it for
     many purposes, from gardening to carpentry.

Introductory Exercises

A.   Match each word or phrase with its definition.

_____ **1.** having many uses or applications

_____ **2.** to anticipate with pleasure

_____ **3.** appropriate according to public standards

_____ **4.** characterized by passionate love

_____ **5.** laughable; foolish

_____ **6.** a very sad or unlucky event

_____ **7.** able to be carried

_____ **8.** an organization of people with a common interest

_____ **9.** a room or building for the showing of art

_____ **10.** to practice for a performance

_____ **11.** a chance

_____ **12.** to cancel

_____ **13.** anger

_____ **14.** one of a series of slightly connected stories or scenes

_____ **15.** balanced

_____ **16.** a sudden, surprising change in a system

_____ **17.** very clever or intelligent

_____ **18.** an open structure made for supporting something

_____ **19.** to invent; to produce

_____ **20.** to suddenly come to exist

_____ **21.** a feeling of very strong love

_____ **22.** a tool for cleaning and painting

_____ **23.** a character assigned or played (usually in a drama)

_____ **24.** to gradually get lower and disappear

_____ **25.** to separate parts of something by force

a. association
b. brilliant
c. brush
d. call off
e. decent
f. die away
g. episode
h. frame
i. gallery
j. look forward to
k. make up
l. opportunity
m. passion
n. portable
o. rage
p. rehearse
q. ridiculous
r. role
s. romantic
t. shock
u. spring up
v. symmetrical
w. tear
x. tragedy
y. versatile

B.   Answer each question with a word from the word form chart.

   1. What tool does an artist use?
   2. What happens to a baseball game if it rains a lot?
   3. Where can you go to see art?
   4. What do actors do before they perform for an audience?
   5. What is around the outside of a picture?
   6. What is something that you can join?
   7. How can you describe a very creative person?
   8. What does a person in love feel for his/her partner?
   9. What is the opposite of a comedy?
  10. How can you describe a hat that has lots of flowers on it and makes you laugh?
  11. What do you do to a pleasant event in your future?
  12. What should you do to a contract that is old and has mistakes in it?

Study Exercises

C.   Write **T** if the sentence is true and **F** if it is false.

   _____   1. People usually associate with people whom they do not like.

   _____   2. Parents want their children to wear decent clothes.

   _____   3. When a sound is dying away, it is getting quieter.

   _____   4. A person who was framed is really guilty.

   _____   5. Portable things are usually very heavy.

   _____   6. A person who can sing, dance, and act well is versatile.

   _____   7. When an event is called off, it occurs slightly later than planned.

   _____   8. An episode is part of a series.

   _____   9. People look forward to tragedies.

   _____ 10. People want many opportunities in their lives.

   _____ 11. People like to appear ridiculous.

   _____ 12. You can get a bad shock if you are too close to lightning.

D.   Complete the analogies with a word from the word form chart.

   1. love : passion :: anger : _____

   2. black : white :: _____ : comedy

   3. student : study :: actor : _____

   4. chapter : book :: _____ : series

   5. postpone : put off :: cancel : _____

   6. glass : break :: paper : _____

7. rain : let up :: noise : _____

8. pasture : fence :: picture : _____

9. music : concert :: art : _____

10. invent : machine :: _____ : story

E. Match each two- or three-word verb with its definition.

_____ **1.** hit on

_____ **2.** work out

_____ **3.** try out

_____ **4.** clear up

_____ **5.** look into

_____ **6.** call of

_____ **7.** die away

_____ **8.** make up

_____ **9.** spring up

_____ **10.** look forward to

a. to invent
b. to find the solution
c. to discover by accident
d. to anticipate with pleasure
e. to use experimentally
f. to suddenly come to exist
g. to end successfully
h. to cancel
i. to gradually get lower
j. to investigate

F. In each blank, write the most appropriate word or phrase from the word form chart.

1. The enraged man _____ all of us by tearing up the valuable painting.

2. Everyone agrees that the death of the young actress by sucide was a(n) _____ event.

3. We bought a _____ television so that we could move it from room to room.

4. The author of that episode had to _____ a new ending when the leading actor complained about the original conclusion.

5. She was hired because she is very _____ . They needed someone to do a variety of tasks.

6. The play opens tonight, so the actors were _____ until late last night.

7. He was so enraged that he _____ his contract and threw the pieces at the director.

8. The plans for the new program were _____ when the writers did not produce a good story.

9. She is not a suitable actress for that _____ . She's much to young for the part.

10. His first _____ to appear on national TV was three years ago when a director offered him a part in a(n) _____ of a famous comedy series.

Follow-up

G. Dictation: Write the sentences that your teacher reads aloud.

1. _____
2. _____
3. _____
4. _____
5. _____

H. Answer the following questions.

1. Do you belong to any associations? Explain.
2. What machines do you have that are portable?
3. Explain the best opportunity you have had in your life.
4. Do you ever go to art galleries? Which one is your favorite?
5. What do you find to be shocking?
6. What performer(s) do you consider to be brilliant?
7. Is your furniture arranged symmetrically? Explain.
8. Why might one person frame another for a crime?
9. What was the greatest tragedy in the history of your country?
10. Describe a time when you felt ridiculous.

I. Complete the story.

Monica is a young actress. Today she begins her first TV role in an episode of a popular series. . . .

Environment

Word Form Chart

NOUN	VERB	ADJECTIVE	ADVERB
			ahead
application	apply	applicable	
		applied	
	bring about		
bubble	bubble	bubbling	
cause	cause	causal	
	chop down		
	come about		
contaminant	contaminate	contaminated	
contamination			
controversy		controversial	controversially
	cut off		
debate	debate	debated	
		debating	
detergent			
	die off		
	die out		
ecologist			
ecology		ecological	ecologically
entirety		entire	entirely
fragility		fragile	
irritation	irritate	irritated	
		irritating	
irritant		irritable	irritably
misuse	misuse		
purity	purify	pure	purely
purification			
impurity		impure	

NOUN	VERB	ADJECTIVE	ADVERB
sanitation	sanitize	sanitary unsanitary	
shame shamefulness	shame	shameful	shamefully
shamelessness		shameless	shamelessly
	undergo		

Definitions and Examples

1. **ahead** (a) [in front; before; in advance]

   You can go **ahead** of me if you're in a hurry.
   Some famous scientists were **ahead** of their time.

   (b) [forward]

   The judge went **ahead** with the trial although the witness was sick.
   I am going to go **ahead** with my research and not wait until I have all the information.

2. **application** (a) [the use of a thing or idea]

   I do not know of any practical **application** for this discovery.
   There is wide **application** for man-made fuels.

   (b) [**1-1**: a formal, written request]

   A job **application** should be completed before you get an appointment for an interview.

3. **bring about** {separable} [to cause]

   Powerful medicine can **bring about** a complete cure.
   Peace was **brought about** through negotiation; fighting did not **bring** it **about**.

4. **cause** (a) [a subject or movement to which many people give their support]

   Clean air is a **cause** worth working for.
   Workers paraded in the street to aid their **cause**.

   (b) [**2-6**: to make happen; to bring about]

   What **causes** iron to rust?

5. **chop down** {separable} [to make fall by cutting]

   If you need firewood, you have to **chop down** a tree.
   After the men **chopped** the forest **down**, the animals had no place to live.

6. **come about** [to happen; to occur]

   Most great achievements **come about** through hard work.
   The discovery of new lands often **came about** through luck.

7. **controversy** [a quarrel; a difference of opinion]

   The president's new policy on agriculture is likely to be **controversial**.
   A **controversy** over national borders can result in a war.

8. **cut off** {separable} (a) [to remove by cutting, to break]

   If you **cut** the flowers **off** the plants, there will not be any seeds.
   Please **cut off** any dead leaves.

   (b) [to stop something suddenly]

   My employment benefits will be **cut off** when I stop working.
   The utility company will **cut** my electricity **off** if I do not pay my bill.

9. **debate** [a public argument of discussion or reasons for and against]

   A formal **debate** is a contest of skill in speaking and reasoning.
   Political candidates often **debate** the current issues.

10. **detergent** [a substance similar to soap, used for cleaning]

    Which **detergent** is recommended for automatic dishwashers?
    You can find many varieties of laundry **detergent** in the neighborhood
      grocery store.

11. **die off** [to die, one after another, until all are dead]

    Acid rain is causing the trees in this forest to **die off**.
    The members of that village **died off** as a result of severe malnutrition.

12. **die out** [to stop little by little; to end completely]

    We were cold after the camp fire **died out**.
    His childhood interest in sports is beginning to **die out**.

13. **ecology** [the science that deals with the relation of living things to their
    environment]

    Ecology is a relatively new science.
    Some **ecologists** study the effects of water pollution on fish.

14. **entire** [whole; complete; not broken; having all the parts]

    It lasted two hours, but I watched the **entire** movie.
    I agree with you. You are **entirely** correct.

15. **bubble** [a thin layer of material enclosing air or gas]

    An imperfect piece of glass may contain a **bubble**.
    Water **bubbles** when it boils.

16. **fragile** [easily broken or damaged]

    The old woman's bones were weak and **fragile**.
    We keep **fragile** instruments in a special cabinet.

17. **irritate** [to make something feel sensitive or painful]

> Tight shoes **irritate** my feet.
> Salt is an **irritant** in an open wound.

18. **misuse** [to use for the wrong purpose; to treat badly]

> The **misuse** of land can cause crop failure.
> The injured horse had been **misused** by the farmer.

19. **pure** (a) [not mixed with anything else; without defects]

> My mother's ring is **pure** gold.
> Is there a cheap way to **purify** this waste water?

(b) [with no evil or sin; perfect; innocent]

> It is difficult to live a **pure** and holy life.

20. **sanitary** [free from dirt; promoting good health; preventing disease]

> Poor **sanitary** conditions have caused the spread of many diseases.
> The department of **sanitation** cleans the city streets.

21. **shame** [dishonor; a painful feeling of having done something wrong]

> The criminal felt no **shame** after stealing so much money.
> It is a **shameful** act to invade a peaceful nation.

22. **undergo** [to experience; to go through]

> Tomorrow he will **undergo** an operation to repair his heart.
> Theresa has **undergone** a series of changes in her personality.

23. **contaminate** [to make impure by contact]

> A **contaminated** water supply is unhealthy.
> It is important not to **contaminate** the experimental sample.

Introductory Exercises

A.   Match each word or phrase with its definition.

_____	**1.** free from dirt	**a.** ahead
_____	**2.** having all the parts	**b.** application
_____	**3.** easily broken	**c.** bring about
_____	**4.** without defects	**d.** bubble
_____	**5.** a difference of opinion	**e.** cause
_____	**6.** to stop something suddenly	**f.** chop down
_____	**7.** a public argument	**g.** come about
_____	**8.** to stop little by little	**h.** contaminate
_____	**9.** in advance	**i.** controversy
_____	**10.** to treat badly	**j.** cut off
_____	**11.** to go through	**k.** debate
_____	**12.** a substance used for cleaning	**l.** detergent
_____	**13.** dishonor	**m.** die off
_____	**14.** to make impure	**n.** die out
_____	**15.** to cause	**o.** ecology
		p. entire
		q. fragile
		r. irritate
		s. misuse
		t. pure
		u. sanitary
		v. shame
		w. undergo

B.   Answer each question with a word from the word form chart.

1. What do people believe in enough to give their support to?
2. What science deals with the relation of living things to their environment?
3. What can you use to wash dishes?
4. What should you do to a dead tree?
5. What makes a pure thing dirty?
6. What does an honest man feel when he steals?
7. What do political candidates sometimes do before an election?
8. What does a particle of dirt do to your eye?
9. How can you describe polluted water?
10. What do we call a thing that breaks easily?
11. What is happening to certain animals that are often hunted by man?
12. What is the result when people have different opinions?
13. What type of conditions prevent disease?
14. What do we see in water when it boils?

Study Exercises

C. Write **T** if the sentence is true and **F** if it is false.

_____ 1. Nuclear energy has no practical application.

_____ 2. New developments in agriculture have brought about higher crop yields.

_____ 3. A union tries to advance the cause of workers' rights.

_____ 4. A tree is entirely underground.

_____ 5. Rocks and bricks are fragile.

_____ 6. Dirty air can irritate the lungs.

_____ 7. Pure alcohol is good for you to drink.

_____ 8. Paper manufacturers chop down many acres of trees.

_____ 9. Nuclear weapons are a controversial subject.

_____ 10. Hospitals try to maintain sanitary conditions.

_____ 11. Anthropologists can describe some of the changes that humans have undergone.

_____ 12. Nuclear contamination is not serious.

_____ 13. If you cut off your finger, a new one will grow.

_____ 14. Conservation depends on the misuse of raw materials.

D. Complete the analogies with a word or phrase from the word form chart.

1. fight : hit :: _____ : argue

2. harvest : crop :: _____ : tree

3. strong: thick :: _____ : thin

4. astronomer : stars :: _____ : environment

5. pick : flower :: _____ : branch

6. use : invention :: _____ : idea

E. Circle the word which does not fit.

1. chop down	a tree a forest the vegetation the swamp		**5.** a fragile	relationship glass egg tractor
2. entirely	uninhabited wealth invisible deaf		**6.** sanitary	needle rock instruments conditions
3. pure	agency silver oxygen iron		**7.** undergo	a compensation an operation an investigation a reduction
4. bring about	a cure a result an expert an end		**8.** cut off	a leaf his salary a dormitory the electricity

F. Read the passage and answer the questions that follow.

Inhabitants of our planet earth are faced with some serious issues concerning our ecology. With industrialization and increased population, the fragile ecological balance which existed in earlier times has become stressed. A serious debate is being carried out in
5 many countries on how to balance growth and development with conservation. Some ideas are controversial, but one point is not. Our earth is limited, and if it is contaminated or otherwise shamefully misused, it may not recover in any reasonable length of time. When it comes to pollution of the environment we are
10 truly in one world; contaminants introduced into the air or water in one country easily find their way to others; entire regions and even large bodies of water are at risk.

The specific contamination and other damage to the environment may vary from place to place, and the methods of
15 purifying these regions also vary. Laws which may be applied to prevent certain types of environmental damage are not uniform and may not be popular. The solutions will be difficult to achieve, but respect for the environment can come about if attitudes undergo change and there is a realization that we are all
20 inhabitants of the same small planet.

Write **T** if the sentence is true and **F** if it is false.

_____ **1.** Industrialization and increased population are solutions to the problem of environmental damage.

_____ **2.** Our earth can always recover quickly from any misuse.

_____ **3.** Contaminants do not respect national borders.

_____ **4.** It is not possible for the oceans to be damaged by misuse.

_____ **5.** There is only one method for the purification of contaminated regions.

_____ **6.** Environmental laws are varied and possibly unpopular.

Follow-up

G. Dictation: Write the sentences that your teacher reads aloud.

1. _____

2. _____

3. _____

4. _____

5. _____

H. Answer the following questions.

1. Name some uses for detergents.
2. What is sometimes responsible for the contamination of a city's water supply?
3. What is a popular cause in your country? Does the government support this cause?
4. Name some practical applications for space travel.
5. What is a controversial topic in your country? What is your opinion on this topic?
6. What are some things that can irritate the eyes?
7. How does the ecology of a forest change when a lot of trees are chopped down?
8. How can you remove impurities from silver?
9. Name some activities that would cause you to feel shameful.
10. What would bring about an improvement in the sanitation of your city?

I. Describe the most serious environmental problem in your country. What are the possible solutions?

UNIT
15

Clothing

Word Form Chart

NOUN	VERB	ADJECTIVE	ADVERB
costume	costume	costumed	
	dress up		
fabric			
	fade	faded	
		fading	
	go with		
	have on		
ink			
	let down		
	let out		
nude		nude	
nudity			
order	order	ordered	
orderliness		orderly	
	pick out		
	show off		
stain	stain	stained	
stocking			
synthesis	synthesize	synthetic	synthetically
	take in		
	take off		
textile			
	try on		
utility			
utilitarian		utilitarian	
waist			
	wear off		
	wear out	worn out	

NOUN	VERB	ADJECTIVE	ADVERB
weave	weave (wove, woven)	woven	
		weaving	
weaver			
	wind (wound, wound)	winding	

Definitions and Examples

1. **nude** [naked]

   The baby in the photograph was **nude**; the weather must have been warm.
   Many artists paint **nudes**.

2. **have on** {separable} [to be wearing]

   A person who is nude does not **have** any clothes **on**.
   Everyone **had on** their best clothes at the party.

3. **pick out** {separable} [to choose; to select]

   She looked into her closet and **picked out** a pair of shoes that looked nice with her dress.

   A: What a beautiful ring!
   B: My husband **picked** it **out** for me.

4. **try on** {separable} [to put on (a piece of clothing) as an experiment, in order to find out if it is the correct size and looks nice]

   Most clothing stores have fitting rooms where you can **try** the clothes **on**.
   He **tried on** the shoes, but they were too loose, so he did not buy them.

5. **take off** {separable} [to remove (a piece of clothing)]

   In Japan, people **take off** their shoes before entering a home.
   I had my coat on, but I **took** it **off** because it was too warm.

6. **go with** {separable} [to look good with]

   She is shopping for a new purse to **go with** her new black shoes.

   A: What colors **go** well **with** red?
   B: How about blue?

√ **7. wear out** {separable} (a) [to use something until it becomes old and in bad condition]

> I **wore out** these shoes in only two months; there is a hole in them.
> We spend a lot of money on books because the students **wear** them **out** so quickly.

(b) [to become old and in bad condition]

> These shoes **wore out** in only two months.

8. dress up {separable} [to put on formal or special clothes, usually for some special occasion]

> We always **dress up** to go to church.
> That little boy has his best clothes on; his mother **dressed** him **up** for this celebration.
> Everyone at the party was very **dressed up**.

9. costume [clothes typical of a certain place or time period, worn in play]

> Everyone at the festival was wearing a **costume**, so everyone looked strange.
> The actors in the play were wearing sixteenth-century **costumes**.

10. fade (a) [to lose freshness or brilliance of color]

> The curtains were **faded** from being in the sun.
> Her dark blue skirt was so old that it had **faded** to light blue.

(b) [to gradually lose strength or loudness]

> The music of the orchestra slowly **faded** away.
> As we drove into the mountains, the radio signal **faded**.

√ **11. let down** {separable} [to lengthen] Ex 92

> This skirt is too short; I will have to **let** it **down**.
> That suit needs to be **let down** two inches.

√ **12. let out** {separable} [to enlarge; to make bigger]

> This jacket is too tight; I will have to **let** it **out**.
> As her child grew, the mother **let out** his clothes.

13. **order** (a) [an arrangement]

My mother told me to put my closet in **order**.
Her clothes are all over her room; there is no **order** at all!
The school children were walking in an **orderly** line.

(b) [an arrangement in time]

The **order** of events was the following: first, the man was murdered; then, the murder weapon was thrown in the river.

(c) [2-11: to command]

When there is an emergency, the police often **order** people to stay indoors.

(d) [2-11: in a restaurant, to ask for food or drink]

The waitress took our **order**.

14. **show off** (a) {separable} [to wear or show proudly] 見せびらかす

The children **showed off** their new clothes at the party.
He drove his new car all over town to **show** it **off**.

(b) [to try to attract attention by one's behavior]

The young boys were **showing off** by pretending to be older than they were.
The children at the swimming pool were **showing off** by screaming as they jumped in the water.

15. **stain** (a) [a dirty spot]

The child had grass **stains** on his knees.
The coffee **stain** on my shirt did not come out in the wash.
The juice **stained** the carpet where it fell.

(b) [to color (wood, glass, cloth, etc.) by processes affecting chemically (or otherwise) the material itself]

Many churches have **stained**-glass windows.
After we clean the wood, we **stain** it.

16. **waist** [the narrow part of the body below the chest]

The **waist** of this skirt is too tight; please let it out.
He wore a belt around his **waist**.

17. **utility** (a) [the fitness for some purpose; the usefulness] 有用 有益

You should keep **utility** in mind when you buy your clothing.
The **utility** of this device is doubtful; it seems to serve no useful purpose.
She is very **utilitarian**; she only buys things from which she will get a lot of use.

(b) [1-12: gas, electricity and water for a building]

A: Does the rent include **utilities**?
B: Gas and water are included, but not electricity.

18. **ink** [a colored material (usually liquid) for writing]

> My pen will not write; there is no more **ink**.
> She used blue **ink** to write the invitations.

19. **wear off** (a) [to gradually come off a surface with time and use]

> The paint has **worn off** the fence; we should paint it again.
> This ink does not wash off my hand; I will have to wait for it to **wear off**.

> (b) [to gradually disappear in effect]

> When the drug **wears off**, the patient will wake up.

20. **take in** {separable} [to make smaller]

> This jacket is too loose; I will ask them to **take** it **in**.
> The clothes fit her well after they had been **taken in**.

21. **wind** [to turn completely or repeatedly about an object]

> He **winds** his watch every morning.
> Her hair was **wound** tightly around her head.
> It is difficult to drive on a **winding** road.

22. **fabric** (a) [cloth or material]

> She bought some cotton **fabric** to make a dress.
> The most common **fabric** for winter clothes is wool.
> That **fabric** will fade when it is washed.

> (b) [an underlying structure]

> The crime problem is damaging the **fabric** of our society.

23. **synthetic** [man-made; not natural]

> Much clothing today is made of **synthetic** fabrics.
> Her job as a chemist is in the production of **synthetic** materials.

24. **synthesis** [the combination of parts to form a whole]

> Chemists work on the **synthesis** of new medicines.

25. **weave** [to make threads into fabric]

> I am making a rug in my **weaving** class.
> This shirt was **woven** by hand in Central America.

26. **textile** [a woven material]

> That **textile** factory produces both natural and synthetic fabrics.
> The United States imports many **textiles** from Asia.

27. **stocking** [a close-fitting covering for the leg and foot, worn by women]

> She wore black **stockings** and black shoes.
> **Stockings** tear easily because they are so thin.

Introductory Exercises

A. Match each word or phrase with its definition.

_p_ 1. man-made; not natural

_q_ 2. to make smaller

_u_ 3. the fitness for some purpose; usefulness

_m_ 4. to wear or show proudly

_h_ 5. to lengthen

_b_ 6. to put on formal or special clothes

_r_ 7. to remove (a piece of clothing)

_j_ 8. naked

_o_ 9. a close-fitting covering for the legs, worn by women

_y_ 10. to make threads into fabric

_z_ 11. to turn completely or repeatedly about an object

_w_ 12. to gradually come off a surface with time and use

_n_ 13. a dirty spot

_i_ 14. to enlarge; to make bigger

_a_ 15. clothes typical of a certain place or time, worn in play

_e_ 16. to look good with

_l_ 17. to choose; to select

_s_ 18. a woven material

_c_ 19. cloth or material

_g_ 20. a colored material (usually liquid) for writing

_v_ 21. the narrow part of the body below the chest

_k_ 22. an arrangement

_d_ 23. to lose freshness or brilliance of color

_x_ 24. to use something until it becomes old and in bad condition

_t_ 25. to put on (a piece of clothing) as an experiment, to find out if it is the correct size and looks nice

_f_ 26. to be wearing

a. costume
b. dress up
c. fabric
d. fade
e. go with
f. have on
g. ink
h. let down
i. let out
j. nude
k. order
l. pick out
m. show off
n. stain
o. stocking
p. synthetic
q. take in
r. take off
s. textile
t. try on
u. utility
v. waist
w. wear off
x. wear out
y. weave
z. wind

B. Answer each question with a word or phrase from the word form chart.

1. What can you write with? *ink*
2. What can you wear if you want to pretend that you are someone else? *costume*
3. What happens to the color of clothes when they are old? *fade*
4. What will juice do to clothing? *stain*
5. What do you do to clothes before buying them? *try on*
6. What do people do for formal occasions? *dress up.*
7. What should be done to clothes that are too big? *take in.*
8. What happens to clothes that you wear often? *wear out.*
9. What must be done to some watches? *wind*
10. What are clothes made from? (two answers) *fabric* *textile synthetic*
11. Around what part of the body do you wear a belt? *waist*
12. What do you do to your clothes at the end of the day? *take off*

Study Exercises

C. Write **T** if the sentence is true and **F** if it is false.

F 1. Men can synthesize gold.

T 2. Weaving is a way to make fabric.

T 3. Your waist size is bigger than your neck size.

F 4. A nude person is wearing a costume.

T 5. People do not want to get stains on their clothes.

F 6. You should dress up to wash the dishes.

F 7. Every piece of clothing goes with every other piece of clothing.

T 8. If a suit is too short, it needs to be let down.

T 9. Clothes which are old may be worn out.

T 10. Most people want to pick out their own clothes.

F 11. People try to show off their worst clothes.

F 12. Parents want their children's clothes to be in order.

T 13. Some textiles are synthetic.

F 14. The utility of all clothing is the same.

D. Complete the analogies with a word or phrase from the word form chart.

_____ 1. man : sock :: woman : *stocking*

_____ 2. size : let out :: length : *let down*

_____ 3. food : taste :: clothing : *try on*

_____ 4. noise : die away :: color : *fade*

_____ **5.** chalk : blackboard :: _____*ink*_____ : paper

_____ **6.** swim : bathing suit :: act : _____*costume*_____

_____ **7.** injured : treat :: _____*nude*_____ : dress

E.   In each blank, write the most appropriate two-word verb from the list.

✓dress up	✓let out	✓take off
✓go with	✓pick out	✓try on
✓have on	✓show off	✓wear out
let down	✓take in	✓wear off

1. The little boy did not want his mother to __*pick out*__ his clothes; he wanted to choose for himself.

2. Because the name of his university, printed on the back of his shirt, was half __*wore off*__ , we could not read it.

3. He wanted to buy the jacket, but when he __*try*__ it __*on*__ , it was too small.

4. Everyone at the graduation ceremony was very __*dressing up*__ .

5. He does not like to wear a tie, and always __*take*__ it __*off*__ as soon as possible.

6. As the children grew, their mother __*take in*__ their clothes.

7. The children wore their old clothes to play in because their mother did not want them to __*have on*__ their new clothes.

8. Those heavy boots do not __*go with*__ that fine party dress; you should wear nice shoes with it.

9. The mother __*let out*__ her older boy's jacket so that it would fit his younger brother.

10. Everyone was __*showing off*__ their best clothes at the party.

11. Even if this dress is __*let down*__ , it will not be long enough.

F.   In each blank, write the most appropriate word or phrase from the word form chart.

Clothing customs among middle-class North Americans have changed significantly in the past fifty years. In the past, the average person bought his clothing primarily on the basis of its (1) __*fabric*__ . Nowadays, people do not expect to wear their clothing for many years, until it (2) __*wear out*__ . The middle class is now concerned with fashion and (3) __*show off*__ their new clothes each year.

Another major change has been in the (4) _____ *Textile* _____ used to
make clothing. Before World War II, most clothing was made of natural
materials, like cotton and wool. But in the years since the war, the use of
(5) _____ *synthetic* _____ fabrics and those that are mixtures of synthetic and
natural textiles has increased greatly.

Another major change has been in the formality of clothing. In the past,
at church or at a party, people (6) _____ *dressed up* _____ in quite formal clothing.
But in the 1980s, people are interested in comfort, so sports shoes are made
to (7) _____ *order* _____ all kinds of clothing. Even at expensive parties,
many guests may (8) _____ *have on* _____ faded jeans and tennis shoes.

Follow-up

G. Dictation: Write the sentences that your teacher reads aloud.

1. _____
2. _____
3. _____
4. _____
5. _____

H. Answer the following questions.

1. Are you an orderly person? Give some examples to support your answer.
2. When do people in your country wear costumes?
3. What kinds of stains are hard to remove from clothing?
4. What is your waist measurement?
5. Does your watch have to be wound? How often?
6. How can you prevent clothing from fading?
7. What colors do you think go well together?
8. Do you pay more attention to utility or to fashion when you buy clothing?
9. Does your country produce textiles?
10. How old were you when you began to pick out your own clothes?
11. Is ink required for your school assignments, or is pencil permitted?

I. Describe the clothing customs in your country. Include answers to the following:

1. What fabrics are used? Are synthetic or natural fabrics more common?
2. What do people do with their old clothes?
3. What kinds of clothing do not go together?

Nature

Word Form Chart

NOUN	VERB	ADJECTIVE	ADVERB
boundary			
bounds			
distinction	distinguish	distinct	distinctly
		indistinct	indistinctly
distinctiveness		distinctive	distinctively
enclosure	enclose	enclosed	
encounter	encounter		
fascination	fascinate	fascinating	
foam	foam	foamy	
		funny	
	give off		
harbor	harbor		
hurricane			
ivory		ivory	
	keep on		
pile	pile	piled	
	point out		
presence		present	
root	root		
ruggedness		rugged	ruggedly
	run across		
	set up		
species			
trail	trail		
trailer			
trunk			
uniqueness		unique	uniquely
vividness		vivid	vividly
	walk back		

Definitions and Examples

1. **enclose** [to surround; to contain; to shut in on all sides]

    The garden was **enclosed** by a high fence.
    The zoo animals were kept in **enclosures**.

2. **foam** [a lot of tiny bubbles]

    Warm beer usually has a lot of **foam**.
    Polluted water sometimes has a **foamy** appearance.

3. **distinct** (a) [not the same; separate; different in kind]

    A fence is **distinct** from a wall.
    Does this animal have any **distinctive** marks?

    (b) [clear; definite; unmistakable]

    A clever child has a **distinct** advantage.
    The mountains are **indistinct** on a cloudy day.

4. **encounter** [to meet]

    I **encountered** an old friend in the library.
    An **encounter** between enemies is unpleasant.

5. **fascinate** [to attract by interest]

    Children are **fascinated** by strange sounds.
    What is the **fascination** of some people for politics?

6. **funny** (a) [strange]

    That's **funny**. The door seems to be unlocked.
    We heard a **funny** noise coming from the garage.

    (b) [1-19: amusing]

    I heard a **funny** joke at a party last week.
    A comedy movie is usually **funny**.

7. **give off** {separable} [to emit; to send out]

    Some substances **give off** radiation.
    Some **give** it **off** more rapidly than others.

8. **harbor** [a safe or protected place, especially for boats or ships]

    The captain put his ship in the **harbor** before the storm.
    I do not **harbor** any bad feelings toward him.

9. **ivory** [a hard, white substance that comes from elephants and is used to make jewelery, etc.]

   Piano keys are usually made of **ivory**.
   Hunters often kill elephants to get the **ivory**.

10. **keep on (with)** [to continue doing]

    You should **keep on with** your work even if it is boring.
    If I had **kept on with** my studies, I would be a teacher now.

11. **pile** [many things lying one on top of another]

    We keep a **pile** of wood near the garage.
    You can **pile** the laundry on this table.

12. **point out** {separable} [to show; to call attention to]

    Could you please **point out** the shelf of reference books?
    The librarian **pointed** them **out** to the new students.

13. **present** [being in a place; not absent]

    Oxygen is **present** in our atmosphere.
    The **presence** of a fever usually indicates illness.

14. **rugged** [rough; uneven; strong; irregular; harsh; severe]

    The original settlers were a **rugged** group of people.
    The land in the far north is **rugged** and isolated.

15. **hurricane** [a tropical storm with strong wind and heavy rain]

    Autumn is the **hurricane** season in the Atlantic Ocean.
    Our home was badly damaged by the **hurricane** last year.

16. **run across** [to meet by chance]

    I **ran across** an old friend in an art gallery last weekend.
    If you **run across** Walter, please ask him to phone me.

17. **set up** {separable} [to build; to begin]

    We **set** our tent **up** near a small lake.
    Do I need a license to **set up** a medical office?

18. **species** [a group of plants or animals that have certain characteristics in common]

    A botanist is familiar with the various plant **species**.
    Did you know that wheat is a **species** of grass?

19. **trail** (a) [a path through a wild or natural region]

> This **trail** leads to a lake in the mountains.
> The animals go south each winter along an ancient **trail**.

(b) [anything that follows along behind]

> The robbers left a **trail** of clues behind them.
> The child **trailed** his broken toy on the ground.

(c) [to follow]

> The police **trailed** the murder suspect for many miles.
> I get tired when I **trail** around after you all day.

20. **root** (a) [the part of a plant that grows downward into the ground]

> Water and food come into a tree through its **roots**.
> Some plants **root** more quickly than others.

(b) [something like a root in shape or position]

> Examples: the root of a tooth; the root of a hair
>
> If the **root** is dead, the dentist will pull the tooth.

(c) [the cause; the source; the origin]

> The **root** of his problem is in his unhappy childhood.
> Some people say that money is the **root** of all evil.

(d) [to be firmly fixed]

> He was **rooted** to the spot by fear.

(e) [to dig with the nose]

> The pigs **rooted** up the garden.

(f) [to support a team or contest enthusiastically]

> The big crowd **rooted** for the Chicago Bears.
> It is more fun to **root** for a winning team.

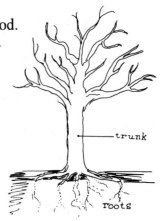

21. **trunk** (a) [the main part of a tree—not the roots or leaves]

> You can discover the age of a tree by examining the **trunk**.
> Tree **trunks** are used to make telephone poles.

(b) [a big, strong box for storing things]

> When I went to college, I sent my clothes there in a large **trunk**.
> My grandmother keeps photographs and letters in a very old **trunk**.

(c) [the long, flexible part of an elephant's face]

> Elephants use their **trunks** to get food.
> An elephant's **trunk** has helped him adapt to his environment.

(d) [the part of a car that is used to hold luggage and other objects]

> A sports car has a very small **trunk**.
> I have an extra wheel in the **trunk** of my car.

(e) [the part of the body to which the head, arms, and legs are joined]

> In this exercise your **trunk** should remain still.

22. **unique** [having no equal; being the only one of its kind; rare; unusual]

    The music of this isolated group of people is **unique**.

    We have developed a **unique** method for preparing beef.

23. **vivid** [bright; lively; strong and distinct; clear]

    The leaves become **vivid** yellow in the fall.

    I have a **vivid** memory of my previous neighborhood.

24. **walk back** {separable} [to return on foot]

    Will you **walk back** to your apartment or take the bus?

    I cannot **walk** all the way **back** by myself.

25. **boundary** [a limiting line]

    A fence forms the **boundary** between my garden and my neighbor's.

    Boundaries are important in many sports; in soccer, for example, the ball must be kept in **bounds** at all times. As soon as the ball goes out of **bounds**, the play stops.

Introductory Exercises

A.   Match each word with its definition.

____ 1. having no equal	**a.** boundary
____ 2. to return	**b.** distinct
____ 3. the main part of a tree	**c.** enclose
____ 4. a path	**d.** encounter
____ 5. to surround	**e.** fascinate
____ 6. strange	**f.** foam
____ 7. to show	**g.** funny
____ 8. the cause or origin	**h.** give off
____ 9. a tropical storm	**i.** harbor
____ 10. a protected place	**j.** hurricane
____ 11. uneven; irregular	**k.** ivory
____ 12. to continue	**l.** keep on (with)
____ 13. not absent	**m.** pile
____ 14. to attract by interest	**n.** point out
	o. present
	p. root
	q. rugged
	r. run across
	s. set up
	t. species
	u. trail
	v. trunk
	w. unique
	x. vivid
	y. walk back

B. Answer each question with a word from the word form chart.

1. What do you walk on through the forest?
2. What part of a tree can a cat climb?
3. What kind of storm causes a lot of damage?
4. What comes from elephants and is valuable?
5. Where can a boat go during a storm?
6. How can we arrange firewood?
7. What part of a tree is under the ground?
8. What do you do when you begin a small business?
9. What is a point of difference between two things?
10. What do you have when you meet someone?
11. What do you call a bright color?
12. What do you have to cross when you go from one farm to another?
13. What does a tour guide do for tourists?

Study Exercises

C. Write **T** if the sentence is true and **F** if it is false.

_____ 1. You should keep on studying even if you're discouraged.

_____ 2. Librarians usually arrange the books in a pile on the shelf.

_____ 3. The leaves of a tree are usually found on its roots.

_____ 4. Coffee is usually foamy.

_____ 5. A fire gives off heat.

_____ 6. A hurricane is a storm with snow and ice.

_____ 7. Numbers and letters should be distinct when you wear your glasses.

_____ 8. Gray is a vivid color.

_____ 9. An elephant's trunk is made of ivory.

_____ 10. The boundaries between countries are referred to as "borders."

_____ 11. You need expert advice if you want to set up a new business.

_____ 12. A direct quote is enclosed in quotation marks.

_____ 13. It's not a good idea to harbor a criminal.

_____ 14. It's a doctor's responsibility to point out the risks of an operation.

_____ 15. There are many species of insects.

_____ 16. Every culture has its own unique customs.

_____ 17. In some sports it is important to keep the ball in bounds.

D. Circle the word that does not fit.

1. national	boundary		**6.** keep on with	your job
regional				the experiment
natural				the homework
expert				the thunder
2. ivory	focus		**7.** a vivid	dream
	merchant			fog
	button			memory
	jewelry			color
3. pile	of wood		**8.** root of a	tooth
	of dishes			tree
	of water			companion
	of clothes			problem
4. give off	heat		**9.** trunk of	a struggle
	light			an elephant
	luxury			a car
	radiation			a tree
5. run across	a friend		**10.** a unique	experience
	an article			solution
	a snake			tree
	a surprise			inch

E. Complete the analogies with a word or phrase from the word form chart.

1. leaf : cell :: _____ : bubble

2. bright : light :: _____ : color

3. airport : airplane :: _____ : boat

4. fur : coat :: _____ : jewelry

5. road : driving :: _____ : walking

6. basement : house :: _____ : tree

7. pole : streetlight :: _____ : tree

F. Read the following passage and answer the questions that follow.

> In 1872 over two million acres of land were restricted by the government for use as a national park. This protected area is in Wyoming and is called Yellowstone National Park. The natural places enclosed within the boundaries of the park are fascinating.
> 5 The region is mainly rugged, with vividly colored mountains and uncounted species of plants and animals. One distinctive sight at Yellowstone is the hot springs. These springs are flows of naturally hot water which come directly from the center of the earth.
> Each year millions of people visit the park for a unique
> 10 vacation. Trained park guides are present to point out the various

trails and also the dangers of a surprise encounter with a wild animal. Some enthusiastic campers like to walk alone into the mountains, set up a tent, and stay for a few days before they walk back again. Some people keep on visiting Yellowstone year after
15   year, and that is understandable.

1. How big is Yellowstone National Park? _____

_____

2. What does the region look like? _____

_____

3. What are hot springs? _____

_____

4. What do park guides do? _____

_____

5. What do some campers like to do? _____

_____

6. Where is Yellowstone? _____

_____

Follow-up

G.   Dictation: Write the sentences that your teacher reads aloud.

1. _____
2. _____
3. _____
4. _____
5. _____

H.   Answer the following questions.

1. How far is the national boundary from your city?
2. What might cause a tree to be uprooted?
3. What things do you find fascinating?
4. Name some places where you might find foam.
5. Describe a hurricane.
6. Name some uses for ivory.
7. What animals are unique to your country?
8. Name some things that give off heat.
9. Are there rugged, unpopulated areas in your country?

10. Describe a vivid memory from your childhood.
11. What do you keep in the trunk of your car?
12. Who should be present at a wedding?
13. What will happen if you do not keep on with your studies?

I. Describe a natural place in your country that is a favorite of tourists.

Family

Word Form Chart

NOUN	VERB	ADJECTIVE	ADVERB
acquaintance	acquaint		
affection		affectionate	affectionately
		alike	
		like	
	blow up		
breakup	break up		
dear		dear	
	drop in		
		grateful	gratefully
hand-me-down	hand down		
harmony	harmonize	harmonious	harmoniously
	hear from		
	make up		
		mutual	mutually
neglect	neglect	neglected	
		neglectful	neglectfully
obligation	obligate	obligatory	obligatorily
	oblige		
offense	offend	offensive	offensively
	part	apart	
portrait	portray		
portrayal			
resemblance	resemble		
sibling			

Definitions and Examples

1. sibling [a brother or sister]

> Many parents want their child to have at least one **sibling**; they feel that an only child will be lonely.
> The question on the psychologist's questionnaire read, "How many **siblings** do you have?" I have one brother, so I wrote "1" in the blank.

2. portrait [a picture of a person]

> A family **portrait** hung on the wall of their living room.
> That artist paints many **portraits**.

3. portray [to show]

> That newspaper article **portrayed** the government official as a criminal.
> Bears are often **portrayed** as dangerous animals, but actually most bears avoid all contact with man if they can.

4. resemble [to look or appear similar to]

> He **resembles** his mother: they have the same dark eyes.
> The **resemblance** between them is quite strong; they look like twins.

5. part [to leave someone]

> The couple **parted** sadly at the airport.
> **Parting** from loved ones is always difficult.
> It is difficult to live **apart** from people that you love.

6. grateful [thankful]

> I am very **grateful** to you for helping me.
> The **grateful** students gave the teacher a gift at the end of the term.

7. acquaintance [someone you know, but not as a close friend]

> I have many **acquaintances** but only two real friends.
> They are **acquainted**, but they do not know each other well.

8. alike [the same; quite similar]

> They are **alike** in their interest in old cars.
> Those twins look exactly **alike**.

9. break up [to end a romantic relationship]

> After a twenty-year marriage, they **broke up** when their daughter went away to college; now they live apart from each other.
> The **breakup** of a marriage is usually very upsetting for the children.
> She is crying because she **broke up** with her boyfriend.

10. **make up** (a) [to become friends again after a period of fighting]

> They did not speak to each other for two weeks, but finally they **made up**.
>
> He argues with her a lot, but they always **make up** soon after.

> (b) [5-12: to invent]

>> The child **made up** a story to explain why he had been late to dinner.

11. **hear from** [to receive communication from]

> I have not **heard from** him for the past two years.

> A: When did you **hear from** her last?
> B: She called me last night.

12. **hand down** [to give to a younger relative]

> The little boy always wore clothes **handed down** from his older brother.
> This old watch has been **handed down** in my family from father to son for four generations.
> Many younger siblings have to wear a lot of **hand-me-downs**.

13. **blow up** (a) [to get angry suddenly]

> My father really **blew up** when I told him I had had an accident with his car.
> My parents **blow up** at me sometimes, but they do not stay angry very long.

> (b) [5-9: {separable} to explode]

>> The building was destroyed when the bomb **blew it up**.

14. **drop in** (on, at) [to visit without warning]

> Let's **drop in at** Grandmother's house on our way home.
> My parents **drop in on** us at least once a week; I wish they would call before they come.
> North Americans rarely **drop in on** friends without calling first.
> We **dropped in at** the restaurant for some coffee after the movie.

15. **offend** [to cause hurt feelings, anger, or difficulty]

> They were **offended** when she did not come to their wedding.
> We thought that his bad language was quite **offensive**.
> When you visit another country and do not understand the customs, it is easy to **offend** people.

16. **neglect** (a) [to give little attention or respect to]

> Those children look **neglected**; their clothes are very dirty, and they look hungry.
>
> Some older people in the United States are **neglected** by their children.

(b) [to leave undone]

> He was fired because he **neglected** his work.
>
> If you **neglect** your studies, you will not graduate.

17. **obligation** [a duty; something that you should do]

> Parents have an **obligation** to take care of their children.
>
> We are **obliged** to pay taxes in this country.
>
> I cannot leave until I have fulfilled all my **obligations** to my company.
>
> The taking of that course is **obligatory** for all seniors.

18. **affection** [an emotion which is less strong than love]

> They have been friends for years and have great **affection** for each other.
>
> She is a very **affectionate** child; she is always kissing people, even ones she has just met.

19. **dear** [highly valued; precious]

> She was a **dear** friend for many years; I was very sad when she died.
>
> He holds that job very **dear**; if he is dismissed, he will be very upset.
>
> My aunt is such a **dear**; she writes us every month and visits us often.

20. **mutual** [directed by each one toward the other(s)]

> Their **mutual** affection is obvious; when they are together, they are always laughing.
>
> They have been **mutual** enemies for years; each hates the other.

21. **harmony** (a) [an internal calm]

> Our family does not live in constant **harmony**; we often have big arguments.
>
> They have a very **harmonious** relationship; they agree on everything and never fight.

(b) [a pleasing arrangement of parts]

> That painting has a lot of **harmony**; it is very balanced.
>
> That singing group is very **harmonious**.

Introductory Exercises

A. Match each word or phrase with its definition.

_____ 1. an emotion less strong than love

_____ 2. to cause hurt feelings, anger or difficulty

_____ 3. to give to a younger relative

_____ 4. to end a romantic relationship

_____ 5. to leave someone

_____ 6. to look or appear similar to

_____ 7. a brother or sister

_____ 8. thankful

_____ 9. to become friends again after a period of fighting

_____ 10. to get angry suddenly

_____ 11. to give little attention or respect to

_____ 12. highly valued; precious

_____ 13. an internal calm

_____ 14. directed by each one toward the other(s)

_____ 15. a duty; something that you should do

_____ 16. to visit without warning

_____ 17. to receive communication from

_____ 18. the same; quite similar

_____ 19. a picture of a person

a. acquaintance
b. affection
c. alike
d. blow up
e. break up
f. dear
g. drop in
h. grateful
i. hand down
j. harmony
k. hear from
l. make up
m. mutual
n. neglect
o. obligation
p. offend
q. part
r. portrait
s. resemble
t. sibling

B. Answer each question with a word from the word form chart.

1. When an artist paints a picture of a person, what is it called?
2. What is something that you should do?
3. Who is someone whom you know, but not well?
4. What do you feel for your friends?
5. What should you do after you fight wiith someone?
6. What are your brothers and sisters?
7. What are clothes that you get from an older sibling?
8. How do you feel when someone helps you?
9. What should parents not do to their children?
10. What do you do to people if you are not polite to them?
11. What is a divorce an example of?
12. What condition do people want within their families?

Study Exercises

C. Write **T** if the sentence is true and **F** if it is false.

_____ **1.** Your uncle is your sibling.

_____ **2.** If you blow up at someone, you should make up later.

_____ **3.** People are usually happy to hear from their friends.

_____ **4.** If someone is dear to you, you will be sad when you have to part.

_____ **5.** Good parents neglect their families.

_____ **6.** Children should be grateful to their parents.

_____ **7.** People usually do not bring up their older siblings.

_____ **8.** Children hand down clothes to their older siblings.

_____ **9.** People want harmony in their family life.

_____ **10.** A good person does not neglect his obligations.

_____ **11.** People usually resemble their acquaintances.

_____ **12.** Couples who are divorced live apart.

D. In each blank, write the most appropriate two-word verb from the list following each sentence.

1. The man was standing on the street and _____ antigovernment information.
   a. handing down   **b.** handing out   **c.** handing over

2. He was _____ by some friends of his parents after they were killed.
   a. brought about   **b.** brought on   **c.** brought up

3. Her car is old and _____ every week.
   a. breaks down   **b.** breaks into   **c.** breaks up

4. They _____ at a bar before they went to the restaurant for dinner.
   a. dropped in   **b.** dropped out   **c.** dropped over

5. This watch was _____ to me by my father.
   a. handed down   **b.** handed out   **c.** handed over

6. His sickness was _____ by his not getting enough rest.
   a. brought on   **b.** brought over   **c.** brought up

7. He is lonely because he has just _____ with his girlfriend.
   a. broken down   **b.** broken into   **c.** broken up

8. Many students _____ of college if they get poor grades.
   a. drop in   **b.** drop out   **c.** drop over

9. His goal as a politician is to _____ positive changes in his country.
   a. bring about   **b.** bring on   **c.** bring up

10. That store has been _____ twice recently. Now they have a guard at night.
   a. broken down   **b.** broken into   **c.** broken up

E. Complete the analogies with a word or phrase from the word form chart.

   1. used : car :: _____ : clothing

   2. die : life :: _____ : relationship

   3. must : necessity :: should : _____

   4. repair : machine :: _____ : relationship

   5. peace : country :: _____ : family

F. In each blank, write the most appropriate word or phrase from the word form chart.

   Many people feel that the perfect family is one which is always harmonious; however, psychologists tell us that the ability to (1) _____ after having an argument is far more important to the health of a family than the ability to avoid arguments entirely. Some families even have frequent loud arguments in which members of the family mutually (2) _____ each other. Such situations are very common among (3) _____ who are of approximately the same ages. But the important thing is not that one family member is (4) _____ by the conduct of another and gets angry. As long as the two family members do not (5) _____ to solve their problem and apologize for their offenses, the family relationship may be strengthened by the incident.

   Therefore, parents who are bringing up children should not be too upset when they fight and should just be (6) _____ when they make up. They should remember that it is easy for people who are only (7) _____ and live apart to avoid problems in their relationships. However, the presence of love and affection within a family often leads to emotional arguments. Therefore, parents should not feel (8) _____ to stop each fight between their children before it starts.

Follow-up

G.   Dictation: Write the sentences that your teacher reads aloud.

1. _____

2. _____

3. _____

4. _____

5. _____

H.   Answer the following questions.

1. Do people in your country drop in on friends? On acquaintances? Explain.
2. Whom in your family do you most resemble? In what way do you resemble that person?
3. Have you ever worn hand-me-down clothes? Whom did they belong to before you?
4. Is there a problem with child neglect in your country? Explain.
5. How do you make up with a friend after an argument?
6. How many siblings do you have? How many are brothers and how many are sisters?
7. If you live apart from your family, how often do you hear from them?
8. What obligations do you feel you have to your family?
9. How can you avoid offending people when you travel to a foreign country?

I.   Discuss the practice of divorce in your country.

1. How often does it occur? Under what conditions?
2. What happens to the children?

Vacation

Word Form Chart

NOUN	VERB	ADJECTIVE	ADVERB
applause	applaud	applauding	
assumption	assume	assumed	
checkout	check out		
	clap	clapping	
	close down		
	close up		
	come along		
concentration	concentrate	concentrated	
correspondence	correspond	corresponding	
desire	desire	desirous	
	do without		
	entitle	entitled	
feast	feast		
feature			
		idle	idly
lease	lease	leased	
	mean to		
mobility		mobile	
		immobile	
pest			
precedent	precede	preceding	
rip	rip		
	see off		
silliness		silly	
stage	stage		
trash			
visibility		visible	visibly
invisibility		invisible	invisibly

Definitions and Examples

1. **rip** [to tear]

> I **ripped** my dress when I was getting out of the car. Do you have a needle and thread?
> She **ripped** the paper in half and threw it away.

2. **silly** [foolish; not serious]

> Taking a walk in this storm is a **silly** idea; you cannot be serious!
> The teacher got angry because the children continued to laugh and act **silly**.

3. **feast** [a large, good meal]

> We had a **feast** at home yesterday because it was a holiday.
> They ate a variety of foods during the **feast**.
> We **feasted** on the meat and vegetables served to us.

4. **clap** (a) [to hit one's hands together to cause a loud noise]

> Everyone **clapped** for a long time at the end of the concert.
> When she finished singing, there was loud **clapping**.
> People usually **clap** at the end of a performance which they have enjoyed.

   (b) [a loud sudden noise]

> There was a loud **clap** as the wind blew the door shut.

5. **applause** [approval publicly expressed by the clapping of hands]

> The **applause** was long and loud; everyone had liked the president's speech.
> The people **applauded** enthusiastically as the singer waved to them.

6. **check out** (of) [to pay one's bill and leave a hotel or motel]

> You can wait in the car while I **check out**; it should only take a few minutes.
> **Checkout** in this hotel is anytime before noon.
> You will have to pay for your telephone calls when you **check out of** the hotel.

7. **desire** [to want]

> You can get any food that you **desire** in this hotel by just picking up the phone and calling room service.
> His **desires** are simple: to find a wife and have a family.

8. **lease** (a) [to rent]

    We **leased** a car for the four years we were in California.
    They are **leasing** a house instead of buying one because they will not be living here long.

    > (b) [1-12: a written contract concerning the rental of an apartment]

    We signed a **lease** for a new apartment yesterday.

9. **mobility** [an ability to move from one place to another]

    If we lease a car, we will have more **mobility** than if we depend on public transportation.
    My grandmother lost most of her **mobility** when she broke her leg.
    North Americans are very **mobile**; they often move from one state to another to find good jobs.

10. **visible** [able to be seen]

    The mountains were **visible** in the distance.
    The woman was **visibly** upset; she was crying.

11. **see off** {separable} [to say good-bye to someone who is leaving]

    We went to the airport to **see** our parents **off** on their trip to Hawaii.
    He **saw** his older brother **off** at six o'clock this morning.

12. **close up** {separable} [to close for a time (said of an establishment)]

    That restaurant **closes up** at the end of September each year and then opens up again in the spring.
    The fire caused some damage in that hotel, so they are **closing** it **up** until the repairs are finished.

13. **close down** [to close permanently (said of an establishment)]

    That restaurant **closed down** because the food was bad and they had few customers.
    The fire department **closed** that hotel **down** because they had had too many fires.

14. **concentrate (on)** [to focus one's attention strongly]

    I need a vacation because I have been **concentrating** so much **on** my job.
    Most people have trouble **concentrating** if they are in a noisy area.
    That music is ruining my **concentration**!

15. **concentration** [the relative amount of something present in a liquid or a place; strength]

    The **concentration** of salt in the Dead Sea is very high.
    There is a high **concentration** of apartment buildings around the university.
    Most of the foreign students at that university are **concentrated** in the engineering and computer departments.

16. **assume** (a) [to take as true]

>   When the teacher saw the two students talking during the exam, she **assumed** that they were discussing the answers and got angry.
>   The thief's **assumption** that the house would be empty was wrong, and the owners called the police.

    (b) [to take the responsibility of doing something]

>   The assistant **assumed** the manager's duties while he was in the hospital.

17. **come along** [to come with someone]

>   When I went to the park, my sister **came along** too.
>   Children are not allowed to **come along** to class with their parents.

18. **do without** [to live without something that you normally have]

>   If we do not have the money, we will have to **do without** a vacation this summer.
>   Man cannot **do without** water for very long.
>   When he was a child, his family was very poor, and he had to **do without** many things.

19. **correspond** (a) [to communicate by letters]

>   I **correspond** weekly with my sister, who is away at college.
>   He is studying through a **correspondence** school; the school sends him lessons, and he studies them and mails in his assignments.

    (b) [for each member of one group to have an association with each member of another group]

>   This intersection **corresponds** to that mark on the map.

>   A: Does your language have a word which **corresponds** to "the" in English?
>   B: No. It doesn't.

20. **entitle** [to give proper power for getting something]

>   This ticket **entitles** you to enter the amusement park and stay all day.
>   All students are **entitled** to use the library and the athletic facilities.

21. **mean to** (a) [to intend to]

>   On our vacation this year, we **mean to** drive all the way across the country.
>   After she graduates, she **means to** get a job as an engineer.
>   I **meant to** finish the work yesterday, but I did not have enough time.

    (b) **mean** [assumed: to indicate; to show]

>   "Gracias" **means** "thank you" in Spanish.

    (c) **means** [5-5: something useful or helpful to reach a goal]

>   We do not yet have the **means** to cure that disease.

22. **precede** [to come before]

> January **precedes** February.
> We took the five o'clock flight because the **preceding** flights were all full.

23. **precedent** [something that can be used as an example for a later, similar situation]

> I asked the professor if I could drop out of the course, but he refused because there was no **precedent** for such an action; no one had ever dropped out of that class before.

24. **stage** (a) [a raised platform for the purpose of public performances, speeches, etc.]

> The room was dark, but there were lights on the **stage** so that we could see the actors plainly.

(b) [a period or step in a process, activity, or development]

> The first **stage** of the construction of the bridge will be difficult; we must be sure that the ground is firm enough to support the bridge.

25. **feature** (a) [a distinct aspect]

> The best **features** of that area of the country are the beaches and forests.

(b) [the appearance of the face and its parts]

> She has the same **features** as her father.

(c) [a special attraction]

> We saw two short movies before the **feature** movie began.
> He is a **feature** writer for a monthly magazine about the city.

26. **idle** (a) [not occupied or employed]

> That factory is **idle** now; they do not have any orders to work on.
> I want to keep busy during my vacation; I do not like to be **idle**.

(b) [not useful]

> You should not waste time on **idle** talk while you are working.

27. **pest** (a) [a plant, animal, or insect which is harmful to man]

> Garden **pests** damaged many of the vegetables that I was growing in my garden.

(b) [a person who is a bother]

> My little brother is a **pest**; he will never leave me alone when I want to study.

28. **trash** [something worth little or nothing]

> The city trucks collect the **trash** from our neighborhood every Monday morning.
> My friends do not like that new play; they say that it is **trash**.

Introductory Exercises

A. Match each word or phrase with its definition.

____	**1.** to intend to	**a.**	applause
____	**2.** an important characteristic	**b.**	assume
____	**3.** to communicate by letters	**c.**	check out
____	**4.** to take as true	**d.**	clap
____	**5.** to say good-bye to someone who is leaving	**e.**	close down
		f.	close up
____	**6.** to rent	**g.**	come along
____	**7.** approval publicly expressed by the clapping of hands	**h.**	concentrate
		i.	correspond
____	**8.** to tear	**j.**	desire
____	**9.** foolish; not serious	**k.**	do without
____	**10.** to pay one's bill and leave a hotel or motel	**l.**	entitle
		m.	feast
____	**11.** an ability to move from one place to another	**n.**	feature
		o.	idle
____	**12.** to close for a time (said of establishments)	**p.**	lease
		q.	mean to
____	**13.** to focus one's attention strongly	**r.**	mobility
____	**14.** to come with someone	**s.**	pest
____	**15.** to give proper power for getting something	**t.**	precede
		u.	rip
____	**16.** not occupied or employed	**v.**	see off
____	**17.** to come before	**w.**	silly
____	**18.** a raised platform for the purpose of public performances or speeches	**x.**	stage
		y.	trash
____	**19.** something worth little or nothing	**z.**	visible
____	**20.** an insect or animal which is harmful to man		
____	**21.** to live without something that you normally have		
____	**22.** to close permanently (said of establishments)		
____	**23.** able to be seen		
____	**24.** to want		
____	**25.** to hit one's hands together to cause a loud noise		

B.   Answer each question with a word or phrase from the word form chart.

   1. What do you need in order to study effectively?
   2. Where do actors perform?
   3. What is of little or no value?
   4. What is another word for a large meal?
   5. What do you do after watching a good performance? (two answers)
   6. What do you do after you stay in a hotel?
   7. What may you do if your friend lives in a distant city?
   8. What can you do if you don't want to buy a car, and you need one for a few years?
   9. What happens to a restaurant that doesn't make any money?
  10. What are poisonous snakes?
  11. What must you do if you want something, but cannot have it?

Study Exercises

C.   Write **T** if the sentence is true and **F** if it is false.

   _____   1. Applause is noisy.

   _____   2. When you assume something, you think it is true.

   _____   3. You want to avoid the things that you desire.

   _____   4. If you are entitled to something, you should get it.

   _____   5. It is easy to concentrate on your work in a noisy place.

   _____   6. You see a friend off when he is arriving at your house.

   _____   7. We sometimes laugh at silly actions.

   _____   8. If you describe a person's features, you are describing his or her face.

   _____   9. People enjoy pests during their vacations.

   _____ 10. People like to save their trash.

   _____ 11. When visibility on a road is not good, drivers should drive slowly and carefully.

   _____ 12. When you rip something, you damage it.

   _____ 13. An idle person is very busy.

D.   In each blank write the most appropriate two- or three-word verb from the following list.

check out of	close up	come down with
check up on	come about	do over
close down	come along with	do without

   1. The police _____ the bar because it was owned by a criminal and used as a gambling center.

2. That emergency situation _____ because people were not careful enough.

3. During the war, people had to _____ many of the imported foods that they were accustomed to.

4. We have to _____ the hotel by 1:00 p.m.

5. If the painting is not done carefully, you will have to _____ it _____ .

6. That ski area is _____ for nine months out of every year.

7. I have a lot of responsibility in my job, but my boss _____ me regularly.

8. Everyone in the family_____ food poisoning after they ate that fish dinner.

9. The family dog _____ the children to the school, but the teacher is making him wait outside.

E.   Complete the analogies with a word or phrase from the word form chart.

1. hunger : starvation :: eat : _____

2. doctor : hospital :: actor : _____

3. white : black :: _____ : busy

4. start : finish :: follow: _____

5. knife : cut :: hand _____

6. silliness : foolishness :: clapping : _____

F.   In each blank, write the most appropriate word or phrase from the word form chart.

While some working people assume that the perfect vacation should provide a chance to be totally idle, many others use their vacation time to focus their attention on something very different from their normal work activities. Such people feel; that (1) _____ their energy on something unusual is a better vacation than lying (2) _____ in the sun and doing nothing.

In the same way, it is also not a good idea to (3) _____ that everyone's greatest (4) _____ is a luxury vacation. While some people feel that after working hard, they are (5) _____ to feast during their vacations, other people choose to spend their vacations in wilderness areas, where they must (6) _____ most of the luxuries of modern life.

So, whether your idea of a good vacation is to sit in a comfortable chair with pen in hand and to work on your (7) _____ , or to (8) _____ the equipment necessary for a dangerous but exciting new sport and give it a try, you can be sure that there are plenty of other people like you.

Follow-up

G. Dictation: Write the sentences that your teacher reads aloud.

1. _____
2. _____
3. _____
4. _____
5. _____

H. Answer the following questions.

1. Are feasts part of certain holiday celebrations in your country? Explain.
2. What do you mean to do with the English that you are learning?
3. Have you ever performed on stage? Explain.
4. What system does your city or town have to deal with trash?
5. What are the best features of your town or city?
6. What techniques do you use to concentrate when you are trying to study?
7. Tell about a time when you had to do without something.
8. What is your greatest desire?
9. During the applause after a performance, do people in your country clap individually or all together?
10. As a citizen of your country, what are you entitled to?
11. Have you ever made an incorrect assumption? Explain.
12. Whom do you correspond with regularly?
13. Do people in your country commonly lease apartments? Cars?
14. Do people in your country tend to be mobile, or do they stay in one place?
15. In the process of learning English, what stage do you think is the most difficult?
16. What are some typical pests in your country?

Transportation

Word Form Chart

NOUN	VERB	ADJECTIVE	ADVERB
acceleration	accelerate	accelerating	
accelerator		accelerated	
deceleration	decelerate	decelerating	
awkwardness		awkward	awkwardly
	back up		
brake	brake		
	break in		
collision	collide		
curb	curb		
curve	curve	curved	
disaster		disastrous	disastrously
gasoline			
gauge			
gear			
	get in		
	get off		
	get on		
	get out of		
impact			
parallelism		parallel	
peak	peak		
	strike		
	(struck, struck)		
velocity			
violation	violate		
violator			
whistle	whistle	whistling	

Definitions and Examples

1. **gasoline** {informal: gas} [a liquid fuel used in cars]

   My car ran out of **gasoline** today and stopped in the middle of the highway. I had to walk to a **gas** station to buy a can of **gas** and then carry it back to the car.

2. **velocity** [a speed]

   The **velocity** of the speeding cars was too great for them to stop before hitting the wall.
   Rockets can escape the earth's atmosphere because they travel at a very high **velocity**.

3. **whistle** (a) [a small device which a person blows into to produce a high, loud noise]

   The policeman blew his **whistle** when he saw the car go through the red light.
   The sound of the lifeguard's **whistle** warned the swimmers that they were in rough water.

   (b) [to use your mouth to produce a high, musical noise, or music]

   The man **whistled** at a pretty girl.
   He was **whistling** a familiar song.

4. **strike** (a) [to hit]

   The car **struck** the small child and killed her.
   The bell rang when the clock **struck** three o'clock.

   (b) [3-24: a situation in which workers as a group refuse to work]

   When the company did not increase their wages, the workers went on **strike**.

5. **accelerate** [to increase the speed or velocity of]

   The car **accelerated** as it went through the intersection.
   You press the **accelerator** in order to make the vehicle **accelerate**.
   When driving, you should **decelerate** before turning.

6. **back up** {separable} [to move in a backward direction]

   You should look in the mirror as you carefully **back up** the car.
   You cannot drive the car any further forward; you will have to **back** it **up**.

7. **brake** [a device for stopping a vehicle]

   The **brake** pedal is to the left of the accelerator.
   The **brakes** failed, and the car struck a building.
   She **braked**, and the truck gradually slowed down.

8. **peak** (a) [to reach a maximum]

> Traffic here **peaks** at about 8:30 A.M.
> The **peak** travel period to Florida is the month of December.
> His **peak** speed during the race was 200 miles per hour.

(b) [the top of a hill or a mountain]

> They climbed to the **peak** of the mountain.

9. **impact** [the striking of one body or thing against another]

> The **impact** of the car accident knocked the driver unconscious.
> We had an accident this morning, but the **impact** was slight, and our car
> was not damaged.
> The president's speech had a big **impact** on the attitudes of the people;
> many of them have changed their minds.

10. **collide** [to come together with solid impact]

> The two cars **collided** in the center of the intersection.
> The **collision** resulted in the deaths of both drivers.

11. **disaster** [an event bringing great damage or loss]

> The town has taken a long time to recover from the **disaster** of the flood.
> The death of the father was a **disaster** for that family.

12. **break in** {separable} (a) [to use (something) until it is comfortable or in good
condition for use]

> I do not want to wear these new shoes to walk to work until I **break**
> them **in**.
> He wants to **break in** his new car by taking some easy drives in it before
> he uses it for a long trip.

(b) [5-10: to go into a building by force]

> The robbers **broke into** the bank during the night.

13. **awkward** [lacking skill or ease; causing embarrassment]

> She felt very **awkward** when she slipped on the ice and fell.
> He got on the horse **awkwardly** because it was his first try.
> It was an **awkward** situation when I met my old boyfriend on the street
> because our break-up had been unpleasant.

14. **get in (to)** [to enter an elevator or a small vehicle such as a car or taxi]

> We **got in** the taxi and went to the airport.
> Six people **got into** the elevator on the second floor.

15. **get on** [to enter an elevator or a large vehicle such as a bus, plane, or train]

> We **got on** the bus in front of our house.
> They **got on** the train and easily found seats.

16. **get out of** [to leave an elevator or a small vehicle such as a car or taxi]

    She **got out of** the car and entered the building.
    Everyone **got out of** the taxi in front of the restaurant.

17. **get off** [to leave a large vehicle such as a bus, plane, or train]

    When we **got off** the plane, we went to get our luggage.
    Watch your step as you **get off** the bus.

18. **curve** [to take a turn or change from a straight line without a sharp angle]

    The road **curves** around the lake.
    There are many accidents at that **curve** in the road when it is icy.

19. **gauge** (a) [an instrument for or a means of measuring or testing]

    The gas **gauge** says "empty"; we had better stop at a gas station.
    I used the pressure **gauge** to measure how much air was in the tires.

    (b) [to measure; to estimate; to judge]

    I **gauged** his performance to be the best.

20. **gear** (a) [one of two or more adjustments of part of the motor of a vehicle that changes its relative speed and direction]

    He put the car in second **gear** to go up the hill.
    Changing **gears** was the hardest part of learning to drive.

    (b) [equipment]

    He took his fishing **gear** to the pond and spent the day there.
    The campers had to carry all their **gear** on their backs.

21. **parallel** (a) [lines extending in the same direction and everywhere equally distant]

    First Street is **parallel** to Second Street.
    She drew two **parallel** lines on her paper.

    (b) [similar]

    The two cultures developed along **parallel** lines and share many similarities.

22. **violate** [to not pay attention to a rule or law]

    The policeman stopped her for **violating** a traffic law.
    If you have too many traffic **violations**, you will lose your license.

23. **curb** (a) [a raised edge on a street, often made of concrete]

    He was parked too far from the **curb**, and the policeman gave him a ticket.
    She stood on the **curb** and waited to cross the street.

    (b) [to control]

    The child could not **curb** her curiosity and opened the present before her birthday.
    You should **curb** your anger when you are speaking to the boss.

Introductory Exercises

A. Match each word or phrase with its definition.

_____ 1. equipment

_____ 2. a raised edge on a street often made of concrete

_____ 3. to take a turn or change from a straight line without a sharp angle

_____ 4. lacking skill or ease; causing embarrasment

_____ 5. to come together with solid impact

_____ 6. a device for stopping a vehicle

_____ 7. to hit

_____ 8. a liquid fuel used in cars

_____ 9. everywhere equally distant

_____ 10. an instrument for or a means of measuring or testing

_____ 11. to enter a small vehicle such as a car

_____ 12. an event bringing great damage or loss

_____ 13. to reach a maximum

_____ 14. to increase the speed or velocity of

_____ 15. a small device which a person blows into to produce a high, loud noise

_____ 16. to move in a backward direction

_____ 17. the striking of one body or thing against another

_____ 18. to use (something) until it is comfortable or in good condition for use

_____ 19. to enter a large vehicle such as a bus

_____ 20. to not pay attention to a rule or law

_____ 21. to leave a small vehicle such as a car

_____ 22. to leave a large vehicle such as a bus

_____ 23. a speed

a. accelerate
b. awkward
c. back up
d. brake
e. break in
f. collide
g. curb
h. curve
i. disaster
j. gasoline
k. gauge
l. gear
m. get in(to)
n. get off
o. get on
p. get out of
q. impact
r. parallel
s. peak
t. strike
u. velocity
v. violate
w. whistle

B. Answer each question with a word from the word form chart.

1. What happens when two cars hit each other? (two answers)
2. What do most cars use as fuel?
3. What must you change when you want your car to go backwards?
4. What are floods and epidemics examples of?

5. What do you look at to see how much gasoline is left in your car?
6. How do you feel if you slip and fall down in front of a group of people?
7. What is at the edge of many streets?
8. What is the highest point of a mountain?
9. What does a driver use to decelerate?
10. What must you do to new shoes so that they will be comfortable?
11. What do criminals do to the law?
12. What must you do to your appetite if you want to lose weight?

Study Exercises

C. Write **T** if the sentence is true and **F** if it is false.

——— 1. Parallel streets intersect.

——— 2. Old things need to be broken in.

——— 3. Policemen who are directing traffic often use whistles.

——— 4. An accelerating vehicle is gaining speed.

——— 5. Brakes are used for acceleration.

——— 6. People who violate the law may go to prison.

——— 7. Gasoline is frequently used to heat homes.

——— 8. When there is a collision, there is an impact.

——— 9. The gas gauge in a car tells us how much fuel we have remaining.

——— 10. All roads have curbs.

——— 11. The streets are crowded with cars during the peak traffic hours in most cities.

——— 12. It is a good idea to accelerate when going around a curve.

——— 13. People enjoy feeling awkward.

D. In each blank, write the most appropriate two- or three-word verb from the following list.

get away	get off	break down
get away with	get on	break in
get by (on)	get on with	break into
get in(to)	get out of	break up

1. When my car ———————————— on the highway, I had to wait for an hour before help came.

2. She chose to ———————————— her project instead of taking a vacation.

3. They ———————————— their rented car and drove to their hotel.

4. I like to sleep for eight hours each night, but if I have to, I can _____ only four hours.

5. These shoes are not comfortable yet; they need to be _____ .

6. They _____ after five years of marriage.

7. The criminals _____ after they had _____ the house.

8. His parents were waiting for him when he _____ the plane.

E. Complete the analogies with a word or phrase from the word form chart.

1. get in : car :: _____ : train

2. fortune : happiness :: _____ : unhappiness

3. food : person :: _____ : car

4. get out of : taxi :: _____ : plane

5. person : get used to :: machine _____

6. good : bad :: skillful : _____

7. furnace : heat :: accelerator : _____

8. car : vehicle :: thermometer : _____

F. In each blank, write the most appropriate word or phrase from the word form chart.

A disastrous collision between two cars occurred at 10:08 P.M. last night on a local mountain road. The drivers of both cars were killed despite the efforts of rescue workers to save them. Witnesses said that both cars were accelerating as they approached the dangerous (1) _____ where the accident occurred. As the two cars approached from opposite directions, neither driver began to (2) _____ until it was too late to (3) _____ sufficiently to handle the curve adequately and stay in his lane. The two cars (4) _____ head on while traveling at high (5) _____ . The force of the (6) _____ was so great that the sound of the collision was heard as far away as the (7) _____ of the mountain by campers spending the night there. The campers hurried down the mountain road to the scene of the accident, but on arriving at the scene discovered that (8) _____ had leaked from the vehicles and caught fire.

Follow-up

G. Dictation: Write the sentences that your teacher reads aloud.

1. _____

2. _____

3. _____

4. _____

5. _____

H. Answer the following questions.

1. Has your country suffered any disasters recently? Explain.
2. When do you feel awkward?
3. What are the peak traffic hours in your city?
4. For what purposes are whistles used in your country?
5. How much does gasoline cost now in your country?
6. Do car owners in your country have to have their brakes inspected? How often?
7. What are the most common violations of the law in your country?
8. What is the proper behavior in your country when a person gets on an elevator?
9. Name something you own that had to be broken in. How did you do it?
10. Name something that has happened recently in your country that had a great impact on many people.

I. Describe a traffic accident that you have witnessed or heard about.

Sports

Word Form Chart

NOUN	VERB	ADJECTIVE	ADVERB
cheat	cheat		
cheater			
	close in		
	count out		
dare	dare	daring	
determination		determined	determinedly
	fall back on		
fellow		fellow	
fellowship			
fierceness		fierce	fiercely
fury		furious	furiously
gaze	gaze		
	go in for		
	go on		
grip	grip	gripping	
heart		hearty	heartily
		heartless	heartlessly
intensity		intense	intensely
	live down		
	look up to		
odds			
program	program		
rival	rival	rival	
rivalry			
roar	roar		
sweat	sweat	sweaty	
		temporary	temporarily
tie	tie		
tournament			
vigor		vigorous	vigorously

Definitions and Examples

1. **cheat** [to trick; to play or do business in a way that is not honest]

   I do not like to play cards with people who **cheat**.
   He failed the test because he was caught **cheating**.

2. **close in (on)** [to come nearer to]

   The hunters **closed in on** the wild jungle cat.
   The army moved at night to **close in on** the enemy.

3. **count out** {separable} [to not consider or include]

   David is always late, so we **counted out** the possibility that he would
       arrive on time today.
   Do not **count** me **out**; I am not tired yet.

4. **dare** (a) [to have courage; to be brave enough to face]

   He does not **dare** to jump off the cliff.
   Early explorers **dared** the unknown oceans.

   (b) [challenge]

   I **dare** you to jump over the fence.
   He was too wise to accept such a **dare**.

5. **go on (with)** [to continue]

   Go on with your game. I do not want to interrupt.
   I cannot **go on with** this story. It is too sad.
   After walking for four hours, the man was very tired and decided to rest
       before **going on**.

6. **grip** [to hold firm]

   Some sports equipment requires a special **grip**.
   The city was **gripped** by a terrible snowstorm.

7. **heart** (a) [courage; feelings and emotions]

   Do not lose **heart**. The game is not finished yet.
   It takes a person with a big **heart** to work with sick children.

   (b) [3-19: the part of the body that moves the blood]

   Heart disease can result in death.

8. **heartless** [having no feelings of sympathy]

   Only a **heartless** person would hurt an animal.
   It is **heartless** to expect so much work from a very old person.

9. **hearty** [friendly and enthusiastic; strong, healthy, and active]

   A working man needs a **hearty** meal.
   His friends gave him a **hearty** greeting when he returned.

10. **fierce** [wild; very strong]

   A **fierce** wind is likely to accompany a hurricane.
   Even a small dog can be very **fierce** if you make him angry.

11. **furious** [very angry; raging]

   Anne's father was **furious** when she came home after midnight.
   The sailors were not prepared for the **fury** of a storm at sea.

12. **gaze** [to give a long, steady look; to stare]

   Lovers often **gaze** into each other's eyes.
   Astronomers use telescopes to **gaze** at the stars.

13. **go in for** [to try to do; to get pleasure from; to enjoy]

   Athletes usually **go in for** nutritious meals.

   A: What sports do you **go in for**?
   B: Swimming and tennis.

14. **intense** [very deep, strong or forceful; fierce]

   In tropical countries the heat is often **intense**.
   The **intensity** of the snowstorm made travel difficult.

15. **live down** [to remove the shame of a mistake or fault by not repeating it]

   Francine was afraid she would never **live down** being late for the meeting.
   It took Mr. Lewis a long time to **live down** his reputation as a liar.

16. **look up to** [to honor or respect; to think of as a good example]

   Bobby always **looked up to** his older brother.
   I am trying to be the kind of boss that the workers will **look up to**.

17. **odds** {plural} [the chance that a particular thing will happen]

   You should know the **odds** before you bet on a horse.

   A: What are the **odds** of your team winning the prize?
   B: Not good—three-to-one against.

18. **program** (a) [a list of the order of events at a show, concert, or meeting]

   Aren't you going to sing at the concert? I don't see your name on the
   program.
   Susan's mother saved the **program** from Susan's graduation ceremony.

   (b) [**1-9**: a show]

   I like to watch sports **programs** on television.

19. **rival** [a competitor; someone who tries to do as well as, or better than another]

   They were **rivals** for the position of chairman.
   No land animal can **rival** the elephant for size and strength.

20. **roar** [a loud, deep sound or noise]

> The wild animals **roared** at the hunters from a distance.
> The **roar** of the traffic was terrible at ground level.

21. **sweat** [the salty liquid that comes out through the skin]

> All this exercise has made me **sweat**.
> **Sweaty** sports clothing should go directly into the washing machine.

22. **determination** (a) [a strong and firm purpose or intention]

> A winning team needs both skill and **determination**.

> (b) [2-24: to find an answer or explanation]

>> Scientists have **determined** the approximate age of many ancient buildings.

23. **fall back on** [to turn to for help or in a time of need]

> I have a small bank account that I can always **fall back on**.
> If I lose my job at the hospital, I can **fall back on** my training as a dancer.

24. **fellow** [a man or boy; an associate, an equal]

> The **fellows** on my baseball team are proud of our record.
> Dr. Fisher went to the conference with his **fellow** physicists.

25. **fellowship** [a group of equals or friends who share similar interests or friendship]

> A good feeling of **fellowship** can come from successful team work.

26. **tie** [an equal score or vote]

> Some games can end in a **tie**.
> The vote is **tied** now. Your vote can break the **tie**.

27. **tournament** [a contest among several individuals or teams in which they compete until only one is the winner]

> An international tennis **tournament** lasts several weeks.
> Tickets for a professional basketball **tournament** are difficult to get.

28. **vigorous** [having physical energy or strength]

> Only a **vigorous** person can work as a miner.
> A winning team needs **vigor**, skill, and determination.

29. **temporary** [lasting for a short time only; not permanent]

> This job is just **temporary**. I hope to have a permanent job next month.
> I will live in a hotel **temporarily** until I find an apartment.

Introductory Exercises

A. Match each word with its definition.

_____ 1. having physical energy

_____ 2. to trick

_____ 3. to hold firm

_____ 4. to have courage

_____ 5. very angry

_____ 6. a list of events

_____ 7. an equal score

_____ 8. to fail to consider

_____ 9. a man or boy

_____ 10. not permanent

_____ 11. to honor or respect

_____ 12. to stare

_____ 13. a competitor

_____ 14. a strong purpose

_____ 15. a loud, deep sound

a. cheat
b. close in (on)
c. count out
d. dare
e. determination
f. fall back on
g. fellow
h. fierce
i. furious
j. gaze
k. go in for
l. go on (with)
m. grip
n. heart
o. intense
p. live down
q. look up to
r. odds
s. program
t. rival
u. roar
v. sweat
w. temporary
x. tie
y. tournament
z. vigorous

B. Answer each question with a word from the word form chart.

1. How can we describe a wild animal?
2. What do we receive at a concert?
3. What do we do when we exercise vigorously?
4. What do two teams compete in?
5. What does a dishonest man do to his friends?
6. What do we call a thing that does not last long?
7. How do we feel when we have been cheated?
8. What do we do when we see a beautiful place?
9. What do we need in order to overcome a big problem?
10. What do we do to someone we think is wonderful?
11. What should we do after we've made a mistake?
12. How can we describe someone who feels no sympathy?
13. What can we call an associate or an equal?

Study Exercises

C.   Write **T** if the sentence is true and **F** if it is false.

_____   **1.** Doctors would like to close in on a cure for heart disease.

_____   **2.** Most people have a rich relative to fall back on.

_____   **3.** It is safe to approach a fierce elephant.

_____   **4.** Sick people often go in for vigorous exercise.

_____   **5.** People usually sweat a lot in cold weather.

_____   **6.** It is a good idea to swim immediately after a hearty meal.

_____   **7.** The odds are good that world hunger will end tomorrow

_____   **8.** A man who cheats makes a lot of enemies.

_____   **9.** Early space travelers dared the unexplored atmosphere.

_____   **10.** Determination is important in business success.

_____   **11.** You should go on with your studies even if you are discouraged.

_____   **12.** If you lose heart, you have a better chance to win the tournament.

_____   **13.** The color of this page is intense.

_____   **14.** It takes many years to live down a big mistake.

_____   **15.** Team members have a feeling of fellowship.

D.   Circle the word or phrase which does not fit.

1. intense	heat dimension color emotion	**5.** gaze	at her voice at his lover at the moon into her eyes
2. the roar of the	engines crowd elements trains	**6.** go in for	vigorous exercise loud music chemical properties expensive clothes
3. cheat	at money at cards on your taxes on the test	**7.** grip	the fork the angle the handle the hammer
4. fall back on	your savings your education your skills the immigrant	**8.** go on with	the concert the calorie your job the trip

9. look up to   the chairman
                       the king
                       the disaster
                       the champion

11. close in on   your goal
                        the solution
                        the enemy
                        the music

10. a fierce   storm
                       dog
                       damage
                       competitor

E. Complete the analogies with a word or phrase from the word form chart in this unit.

1. _____ : screwdriver :: hold : baby

2. _____ : animal :: scream : child

3. _____ : team :: enemy : army

4. _____ : concert :: menu : restaurant

5. _____ : vote :: equal : weights

6. _____ : color :: volume : sound

F. Read the passage and answer the questions that follow.

Good evening, sports fans, and welcome to the second game of the National Basketball Association tournament. The Boston Celtics and the Los Angeles Lakers have just finished the first half of the second game. The Celtics won the first game, and the score

5   is tied now. The odds are in favor of another Celtic win, but the Lakers certainly can't be counted out yet. They are daring and determined, and they would never be able to live it down if they lost one more game. However, if the Celtics do go on to win this game, they will close in on another championship.

10   The teams have just returned to the court. The players are sweaty, and the crowd is roaring. The fans are gripping their programs tightly as they gaze at the clock and anticipate the start of the second half. Do the Lakers have the heart to defeat the Celtics, or will we be looking up to a new champion? There's the

15   signal, and the second half has started.

1. What sport is being played? _____

_____

2. What are the names of the rivals? _____

_____

3. Who won the first game? _____

_____

4. What is the score in this game? _____

_____

5. Who is favored to win this game? _____

_____

6. What are the fans holding? _____

_____

7. What are the fans looking at? _____

_____

Follow-up

G. Dictation: Write the sentences that your teacher reads aloud.

1. _____
2. _____
3. _____
4. _____
5. _____

H. Answer the following questions.

1. Name a game that cannot end in a tie.
2. What items are listed on a program?
3. Name some animals that roar.
4. What famous person do you most look up to?
5. What activities make you sweaty?
6. What can you fall back on if you lose your job?
7. If you are caught cheating, how can you live it down?
8. Did you ever accept a dangerous dare?
9. What are the odds of a nuclear war occurring in this century?
10. What sports might older people go in for?
11. What do you do when you feel furious?
12. What kinds of jobs are usually temporary?

I. Tell about a sports event that you have attended or participated in.

Fire

Word Form Chart

NOUN	VERB	ADJECTIVE	ADVERB
arson			
arsonist			
ash		ashen	
block			
breeze		breezy	
brightness	brighten	bright	brightly
broom			
	burn down		
	burn up		
charcoal			
chimney			
	drench	drenching	
extinguisher	extinguish		
fireplace			
flame		flaming	
		flammable	
		inflammable	
		nonflammable	
furtiveness		furtive	furtively
glow	glow	glowing	
incendiary		incendiary	
	light up		
match			
morality		moral	morally
morals		immoral	
		amoral	
	put out		
set	set		
spark	spark		

NOUN	VERB	ADJECTIVE	ADVERB
	spot		
	stand by		
stealth		stealthy	stealthily
	sweep (swept, swept)		
	sweep out		

Definitions and Examples

1. **arson** [the crime of intentionally damaging a building or other property by fire]

    Arson was the cause of the fire in the empty garage.
    The police have not been able to catch the **arsonist** who is suspected of starting so many fires.

2. **ash** [what remains of a thing after it has been burned]

    The **ash** from his cigarette fell on the floor.
    I do not like to find cigarette **ashes** on my rug.
    After the big fire in the barn, nothing remained but **ashes**.

3. **block** [a solid piece of wood, stone, etc.]

    Stone **blocks** can be used to mark the edge of a garden.
    I need one more **block** of wood to finish building this bench.

4. **set** (a) [to put in some condition]

    You can **set** the bed on fire if you are careless with cigarettes.
    Many prisoners were **set** free when the new government was elected.

    (b) [to put or place]

    Please **set** the package on this table.
    Would you like to **set** that luggage down? It looks heavy.

    (c) [to adjust or put in the correct position]

    A clock should be **set** to show the local time.
    The doctor **set** the broken bone in Bill's hand.

    (d) [to fix or arrange]

    The city government can **set** the speed limit.
    Have you **set** a definite time for our next appointment?

    (e) [a number or group of things or people that belong together]

    My grandmother gave me a **set** of antique dishes.
    We need a special **set** of tools to fix our car.

5. **match** (a) [a short, thin piece of wood with a special tip, used to start a fire]

   Children should never play with **matches**.
   When you go camping, it is important to keep the **matches** dry.

   (b) [to be alike]

   This dish does not **match** the others in the set.
   Where can I find a **match** for this fabric? It is not a common color.

   (c) [3-21: a game or contest between two teams or two people]

   The tennis **match** was very exciting to watch; it was impossible to say who was going to win until the end.

6. **chimney** [the tall structure in a building used to carry away smoke]

   Chimneys are often built of brick.
   A **chimney** should be cleaned regularly to prevent fires.

7. **furtive** [secret]

   The criminal had a **furtive** manner.
   The members of the gang moved **furtively** into the empty store.

8. **charcoal** [a substance made by partly burning wood or bones]

   Artists sometimes use **charcoal** for drawing.
   Water can be cleaned by forcing it through **charcoal**.

9. **put out** {separable} [to cause a fire to stop]

   Many men were needed to **put out** such a large fire.
   They **put** it **out** with the help of modern fire fighting equipment.

10. **extinguish** [to put out]

    Airplane passengers are usually asked to **extinguish** all cigarettes during landing.
    Special fire **extinguishers** are used to put out chemical fires.

11. **breeze** [a light wind]

    A cool **breeze** is welcome on warm summer nights.
    Fires can grow quickly on a **breezy** day.

12. **stand by** [to be or get ready for use or action]

    Additional fire fighters will **stand by** until they are needed.
    The nurse **stood by** while the doctor examined the baby.

13. **bright** [giving a lot of light; light or clear; vivid]

    The sun is **bright** on a clear day.
    A **bright** fire is pleasant when you're camping.
    Ann wore a **bright** blue dress.

14. **spark** [a small bit of fire]

> A big fire can be caused by a tiny **spark**.
> The gas in your car engine is exploded by an electric **spark**.

15. **stealthy** [done in a secret way]

> The information was discovered by **stealth**. No one else knows about it.
> You must be **stealthy** if you expect to hunt successfully.

16. **glow** [the brightness or the shine from something that is very hot]

> The fire continued to **glow** long after the flames were gone.
> Some natural substances can **glow** in the dark.

17. **flame** [the red or yellow light of a fire]

> The forest fire was so big that the **flames** could be seen for miles.
> The **flame** of a single candle gives only a little light.

18. **flammable** {also: inflammable} [easily set on fire]

> Dry grass is very **flammable**.

19. **nonflammable** [not able to be set on fire]

> Rocks are **nonflammable**.

20. **drench** [to wet thoroughly]

> The garden was **drenched** by a seasonal storm.
> A **drenching** rain discouraged both the players and the fans.

21. **incendiary** [having to do with setting or starting fires or rebellion]

> A bomb is an **incendiary** device.
> You can be arrested for making an **incendiary** speech.

22. **spot** (a) [to see after looking for; to recognize]

> A good teacher will **spot** every mistake.
> It was too dark to **spot** the enemy planes.

> > (b) [3-4: a mark on clothing made by food, grass, coffee, etc.]

> > She used water to remove the **spot** on his shirt.

23. **moral** (a) [good in character, right]

> A man needs discipline to lead a **moral** life.
> Murder is an **immoral** act.

(b) [the lesson; the meaning]

> The **moral** of the story is to love your neighbor.
> There is a **moral** for us in this event; we must be more careful in the future.

24. **morals** [standards of conduct]

> Someone with no **morals** is amoral, and someone with bad **morals** is immoral.
> Parents are responsible for teaching their children **morals**.

25. **fireplace** [a place which is built to hold a fire]

> On snowy days we like to sit close to the **fireplace**.
> Heat-resistant bricks are suitable for making a **fireplace**.

26. **light up** (a) {separable} [to make bright]

> A very large fire can **light** the sky **up** for miles.
> Jeff's face **lit up** when he heard the good news.

(b) [to make a cigarette burn]

> Jack wanted to **light up** his cigarette, but he could not find a match.
> Do not **light up** here. Smoking is not permitted in this building.

27. **broom** [a tool with a long handle that is used for cleaning]

> A **broom** is a useful tool for cleaning floors.
> Some **brooms** are made of plastic, but others are made of natural materials.

28. **sweep** [to clean a floor with a broom]

> Susan **sweeps** the kitchen floor every night.

29. **sweep out** {separable} [to clean the bottom surface of an enclosed place with a broom]

> After the fire went out, I **swept** the ashes **out** of the fireplace.
> You should **sweep out** the trunk of your car before you put your new luggage in there.

30. **burn down** {separable} [to burn completely, usually in reference to large things, such as buildings or forests]

> If you are careless with camp fires, you might **burn** the whole forest **down**.
> The hotel **burned down** because a guest had been smoking in bed.

31. **burn up** {separable} [to burn completely, usually in reference to smaller things]

> We should be careful not to **burn up** all the wood before the end of the winter.
> The police found no clues because the criminal **burned** the papers **up**.

Introductory Exercises

A. Match each word or phrase with its definition.

_____ 1. to destroy completely by fire
_____ 2. a small bit of fire
_____ 3. to put out
_____ 4. done in a secret way
_____ 5. a light wind
_____ 6. used to start a fire
_____ 7. a solid piece of wood
_____ 8. a tool for sweeping
_____ 9. good in character
_____ 10. to wet thoroughly
_____ 11. to get ready for action
_____ 12. vivid
_____ 13. secret
_____ 14. carbon produced by burning
_____ 15. place built for a fire
_____ 16. to clean with a broom
_____ 17. to see
_____ 18. to make bright

a. arson
b. ashes
c. block
d. breeze
e. bright
f. broom
g. burn up
h. charcoal
i. chimney
j. drench
k. extinguish
l. fireplace
m. flame
n. furtive
o. glow
p. incendiary
q. light up
r. match up
s. moral
t. put out
u. set
v. spark
w. spot
x. stand by
y. stealthy
z. sweep

B. Answer each question with a word from the word form chart.

1. What does metal do when it is heated to red hot?
2. What do fire fighters hope to do to a fire?
3. Where does the smoke go when it leaves the fireplace?
4. What do some people use to light cigarettes?
5. Who is the person who starts fires for excitement or profit?
6. What might we use to sweep out the fireplace?
7. What should we do to the camp fire when we are finished with it?
8. What could happen to your house if you have a fire that cannot be controlled?
9. What remains in the fireplace after the wood is burned up?
10. What do you need to put out an electrical fire?
11. What do fire fighters do during the dry season?
12. What can cause a fire to advance quickly?
13. What is the lesson you sometimes learn from a story?

Study Exercises

C. Write **T** if the sentence is true and **F** if it is false.

_____ 1. A fire extinguisher is an incendiary device.

_____ 2. Arson is an immoral act.

_____ 3. A chimney is often made of brick or stone.

_____ 4. You need a telescope to spot the most distant planets.

_____ 5. A small spark from a fireplace can cause a serious house fire.

_____ 6. Stone blocks could be used to build a fireplace.

_____ 7. Wet matches work as well as dry matches.

_____ 8. Charcoal is usually black.

_____ 9. Wood is flammable.

_____ 10. If you don't have an umbrella, you could be drenched in a thunderstorm.

_____ 11. An exploding bomb can light up the whole sky.

_____ 12. The broom is a recent technological development.

_____ 13. If you move furtively, other people might become suspicious.

_____ 14. The sun is the brightest object in our sky.

_____ 15. An electric stove has no flame.

D. Circle the word or phrase that does not fit.

1. burn down	the apartment the house the smoke the city	6. a bright	velocity star light fire
2. set	the table a match a fire the clock	7. a moral	issue judgment decision peninsula
3. spot	the dignity the army the airport the island	8. a breezy	ratio afternoon location March
4. light up	the room the sky the street the arson	9. sweep out	the truck the wall the fireplace the closet
5. a drenching	rain symmetry storm wave		

E. Complete the analogies with a word or phrase from the word form chart.

   1. iron : rust :: wood : _____

   2. robbery : thief :: fire : _____

   3. ice : cube :: wood :_____

   4. sound : loud :: light : _____

   5. wall : wash :: fireplace : _____

   6. professor : teach :: priest : _____

   7. water : drain :: smoke : _____

   8. cut : knife :: clean : _____

   9. start : car :: _____ : fire

F. In each blank, write the most appropriate word or phrase from the word form chart.

      Nine people were injured last night when the Hotel Acene completely burned down. Fire department officials said that the (1) _____ moved quickly because of the breeze, and by ten o'clock the glow (2) _____ the sky. Investigators have not determined the cause of the fire but are looking through the (3) _____ for clues. No (4) _____ device was found, but (5) _____ is suspected. Some guests say they (6) _____ a young man with (7) _____ in his hand walking stealthily through the hall. Other guests complained that not enough fire (8) _____ were available. Fire fighters will (9) _____ for most of today to be sure that every spark has been (10) _____ .

Follow-up

G. Dictation: Write the sentences that your teacher reads aloud.

   1. _____

   2. _____

   3. _____

   4. _____

   5. _____

H.   Answer the following questions.

    1. Name some uses for blocks.
    2. What is the best way to put out a fire?
    3. What is a reasonable punishment for arson?
    4. Where is the nearest fire extinguisher?
    5. How can you make metal glow?
    6. What remains after the fire has been put out?
    7. Name some things that are nonflammable.
    8. Which season is breezy here?
    9. How can we prevent being drenched in a rainstorm?
   10. What things are bright enough to light up the sky?
   11. Who should be responsible for teaching morality?
   12. What problems result after a forest has burned down?
   13. What equipment is useful in spotting unusual birds?

I.   Complete the story.

    Jackie is eight years old. His mother doesn't know he is playing with matches. . . .

Government (B)

Word Form Chart

NOUN	VERB	ADJECTIVE	ADVERB
affair			
affairs			
alien	alienate	alien	
arrangement	arrange	arranged	
	back down		
ban	ban	banned	
	bring off		
census			
	come out with		
corruption	corrupt	corrupted	
		corrupting	
	count on		
dilemma			
		domestic	domestically
exclusion	exclude	excluded	
		exclusive	exclusively
	give out		
	go back on		
institution	institute	institutional	
institute	institutionalize		
justice		just	justly
		unjust	unjustly
menace	menace	menacing	menacingly
prominence		prominent	prominently
propaganda	propagandize		
reverse	reverse		
reversal			
sneak	sneak	sneaky	sneakily
territory		territorial	
unity	unite	united	

Definitions and Examples

1. **give out** {separable} [to distribute; to hand out]

   During the campaign, all the candidates **give out** printed information about themselves.

   The rescuers **gave** blankets **out** to all of the victims.

2. **just** [fair]

   The people are complaining that the new law is not **just** because it favors certain groups over others.

   That judge is known for his **just** decisions.

   Their constitution promises **justice** to all.

3. **sneak** [to go in a secret way]

   The robbers **sneaked** into the house through a rear window.

   There was a **sneak** attack on the capital this morning by enemy troops; the government and the citizens were unprepared for it.

4. **propaganda** [the distribution of information or ideas with the purpose of presenting certain positive or negative attitudes about a person or an institution]

   Most people think that the official government newspaper is nothing but **propaganda**.

   During a war, there is normally a lot of **propaganda** produced on both sides.

5. **menace** [a danger; a threat]

   That criminal is so dangerous that he is a **menace** to all of us.

   The pollution in our atmosphere is a **menace** to our health.

   The disease which is **menacing** our city must be stopped.

6. **prominent** [well known; easily seen]

   She is one of our most **prominent** journalists; many people are familiar with her writing.

   He hung the picture of his family in a **prominent** position on the wall of his office.

   That political party rose to **prominence** after the war; before that, it was not popular.

7. **territory** (a) [a geographical area belonging to a government]

   The government wants to establish more schools in the new **territories**.

   (b) [an assigned area]

   That salesman's **territory** is the western states.

8. **exclude** [to keep out; to not permit to enter]

   The people will rebel if they feel that they are **excluded** from sharing the wealth of the country.

   The **exclusion** of some political parties from the campaign will result in an unjust election.

9. **go back on** [to fail to keep a promise or an agreement]

   He **went back on** his agreement and did not lower taxes as he had promised during the campaign.

   She will not be elected again because she has **gone back on** too many of her promises.

10. **arrange** [to put into proper order or into a correct relationship]

    My job is to **arrange** the president's appointments for each day.

    The **arrangement** of the tables is not suitable for a formal dinner; please change it.

    You should make **arrangements** to visit the library and get the data that you need.

11. **ban** [to censor; to not permit]

    That novelist's books have been **banned** because he advocates revolution against the government.

    Smoking in the elevators is **banned**.

    The **ban** against washing cars and watering lawns will be lifted as soon as we have a heavy rain.

12. **affairs** [public or professional business]

    Many people do not understand government **affairs** very well.

    She committed suicide because her business **affairs** were going badly.

13. **affair** (a) [something causing public worry or controversy]

    The Watergate **affair** has had a major influence on American politics.

    That politician's involvement in that **affair** last year has ruined his political future.

    (b) [a romantic involvement, usually for a short time]

    His wife divorced him when she found out about his **affair** with his secretary.

14. **reverse** (a) [opposite]

    His opinion is the **reverse** of mine; I am in favor of the new law, and he is against it.

    (b) [to turn or move in the opposite direction]

    The mayor **reversed** his previous decision to build a new park; now he says that there is not enough money for another park.

    When she realized she was walking in the wrong direction, she **reversed** her steps.

    The president's **reversal** on the arms negotiations surprised the media; everyone had thought that he would agree to sell the arms, but he refused.

15. **bring off** {separable} [to carry out to a successful conclusion; to accomplish]

> Our party will not be able to **bring off** a victory in the next election unless we gain more public support.
> The enemy has been planning an attack, but they do not have enough troops to **bring** it **off**.

16. **institute** (a) [to establish; to originate]

> The government wants to **institute** some new regulations concerning imported products.
> The **institution** of that song as the official song of our country would please many people.

    (b) [an organization for the promotion of a cause]

> The **Institute** for the Blind helps train recently blinded people.
> He works for a research **institute** that does a lot of medical research.

    (c) [an important custom or organization in a culture]

> Our people have a lot of respect for the **institution** of marriage.

17. **unite** [to put together to form one]

> The new government will have to **unite** the people to be able to rule effectively.
> If those two parties **unite**, our party will not be able to win the election.
> Many people want world **unity** and the peace it would bring.

18. **count on** [to anticipate as certain; to trust]

> She believes that she can **count on** winning the election if we support her.
> You should be able to **count on** your friends' help; if you cannot, then they are not your real friends.

19. **domestic** (a) [of, relating to, or carried out within one's own country]

> The president has good control of **domestic** affairs, but many people think that he does not have enough control in the area of foreign affairs.
> We should try to use more **domestic** products, instead of importing so much.

    (b) [of, relating to, or within the home or the family]

> He has **domestic** problems: he and his wife are always fighting.
> In some cultures the mother has total control over all **domestic** affairs, including how the family's money is spent.

20. **come out with** [to produce; to offer to the public]

> The popularity of that party is growing because they have **come out with** many good ideas recently.
> That author **comes out with** a new novel almost every year.

21. **alien** (a) [relating or belonging to another country; foreign]

   > All **aliens** living in the United States must register with the government once a year.
   >
   > **Aliens** who have entered the country without permission are called illegal **aliens**.

   (b) [strange]

   > She had trouble adjusting to the **alien** customs of her new country's people.
   >
   > He is such a hard worker that taking a vacation is an **alien** idea to him.

22. **back down** [to withdraw from a promise or a position]

   > The president said that he was going to raise taxes, but he **backed down** when he heard the strong complaints of the people.
   >
   > The kidnapper threatened to kill the child, but he **backed down** when he realized that he would be caught and punished.

23. **census** [an official count of the population by a government]

   > The United States government conducts a **census** every ten years.
   >
   > The last **census** showed that many northern cities are losing population.

24. **dilemma** [a problem which seems to have no satisfactory solution]

   > The new government now faces the **dilemma** of the poor economic condition of the country.
   >
   > She is famous for solving difficult **dilemmas**.

25. **corrupt** (a) [characterized by improper behavior]

   > The **corrupt** government official took bribes from certain business executives.
   >
   > The people are angry about the amount of **corruption** in the government.

   (b) [to change from good to bad]

   > People are often **corrupted** by power.
   >
   > The young man had been **corrupted** by his older brother, who was a criminal.

Introductory Exercises

A. Match each word or phrase with its definition.

_____ **1.** fair

_____ **2.** an official count of the population by the government

_____ **3.** a problem which seems to have no satisfactory solution

_____ **4.** to turn or move in the opposite direction

_____ **5.** something causing public worry or controversy

_____ **6.** to carry out to a successful conclusion

_____ **7.** to anticipate as certain; to trust

_____ **8.** to establish; to originate

_____ **9.** well known; easily seen

_____ **10.** to put together to form one

_____ **11.** to distribute; to hand out

_____ **12.** relating or belonging to another country; foreign

_____ **13.** to keep out; to not permit to enter

_____ **14.** to go in a secret way

_____ **15.** to put into proper order or into a correct relationship

_____ **16.** to produce; to offer to the public

_____ **17.** of, relating to, or carried out within one's own country

_____ **18.** a danger; a threat

_____ **19.** the distribution of information or ideas with the purpose of presenting certain positive or negative attitudes about a person or an institution

_____ **20.** to censor or not permit

_____ **21.** to withdraw from a promise or a position

_____ **22.** characterized by improper behavior

_____ **23.** a geographical area belonging to a government

_____ **24.** to fail to keep a promise or an agreement

a. affair
b. alien
c. arrange
d. back down
e. ban
f. bring off
g. census
h. come out with
i. corrupt
j. count on
k. dilemma
l. domestic
m. exclude
n. give out
o. go back on
p. institute
q. just
r. menace
s. prominent
t. propaganda
u. reverse
v. sneak
w. territory
x. unite

B. Answer each question with a word or phrase from the word form chart.

1. What counts the number of people in a country?
2. What type of problem is very difficult to solve?
3. What do people want from a court?
4. What do some governments do to things that they do not like?
5. What is the opposite of "foreign"?
6. What can you call information about another country that is not true?
7. How can you describe a government official who takes bribes?
8. What does a person do when he does not want to be seen?
9. What is something that threatens you?
10. What would a visitor from another planet be?
11. How can you describe important people that everyone knows about?

Study Exercises

C. Write **T** if the sentence is true and **F** if it is false.

_____ 1. We call something alien when we have seen it often.

_____ 2. Governments sometimes ban books which they do not like.

_____ 3. A corrupt judge is only interested in justice.

_____ 4. When you arrange things, you put each one in its proper place.

_____ 5. If people are united, they work together.

_____ 6. Propaganda helps people to see the truth.

_____ 7. People welcome things which menace them.

_____ 8. People respect a person who goes back on his promise.

_____ 9. People are happy when they bring something off.

_____ 10. If you reverse a decision, you have changed your mind.

_____ 11. A stronger person will back down when facing a weaker person.

_____ 12. Criminals sneak about so that they will not be caught.

_____ 13. A prominent person will seldom be recognized.

_____ 14. People usually exclude their friends from their parties.

_____ 15. Domestic products usually carry a heavy import tax.

D. Circle the word which is different in meaning.

1. ban   institute   censor

2. kindness   justice   fairness

3. prominence   importance   insistence

4. exclusion   census   count

5. foreign   alien   corruption

6. arrangement   area   territory

7. problem   corruption   dilemma

8. menace   threat   alienate

E. In each blank, write the proper form of the most appropriate two- or three-word verb from the following list.

back down	go back on
bring off	count out
come out with	go on with
count on	look up to
give out	live down

1. I had thought that I could _____ my parents for help, but they were against my plan.

2. Although they were against the plan, I decided to _____ it and continued my preparation.

3. The government is _____ printed literature concerning the nature of the epidemic.

4. Everyone agrees that the entire population is at risk, but so far

   no one has _____ a practical defense against the disease.

5. The mayor has now _____ his promise to fire all the city employees connected with the recently publicized corruption.

6. The mayor was forced to _____ when the city employees' union threatened a strike if any of its members were fired.

7. Everyone (a) _____ because he was able to

   (b) _____ the peace conference successfully.

8. He will never be able to (a) _____ his reputation as a corrupt

   official. We should (b) _____ him _____ of any future plans.

F. In each blank, write the most appropriate word or phrase from the word form chart.

The history of native Americans in the United States is a sad one following the arrival of the white settlers. At first the native Americans simply moved farther west into (1) _____ that the whites did not yet want. The U.S. government even signed agreements which (2) _____ for the native Americans to be given exclusive rights to certain regions.

Unfortunately, during the nineteenth century, the government (3) _____ almost all of its promises to the native Americans and demanded that they give up even more of their land. Naturally, the native Americans fought to keep what was theirs, and as some white settlers were killed, the whites came to view native Americans as a (4) _____ to their survival. In addition to the reality of the native American–white struggle, the newspapers came out with a lot of (5) _____ which showed native Americans to be (6) _____ and untrustworthy.

More unfortunate, even today the state of native American affairs in the United States is not good. Many of them feel (7) _____ from society, as if they were strangers in a land where they have lived for more than a thousand years. Many feel that the U.S. legal system does not provide (8) _____ for native Americans and that they cannot (9) _____ the U.S. government to help them. In short, the problems of the "first Americans" are a (10) _____ for which the United States has not yet found a solution.

Follow-up

G. Dictation: Write the sentences that your teacher reads aloud.

1. _____

2. _____

3. _____

4. _____

5. _____

H.   Answer the following questions.

1. Does your country have a census? How often? Is it considered to be accurate? Why or why not?
2. Name a recent public affair that caused embarrassment to a government.
3. Are there any special laws concerning aliens living in your country? Explain.
4. Are there research institutes in your country? Explain.
5. Who are the most prominent politicians in your country?
6. Does your country own any territory that is not physically connected to the rest of the country?
7. What is the greatest dilemma facing your country today?
8. Has your government recently reversed any of its decisions? Explain.
9. What countries can your country count on if international disagreements occur?
10. Are any groups excluded from voting in elections in your country?

I.   Congratulations! You have just graduated from the university. You feel that you can help your country most if you become active in politics. How would you start? What arrangements would you make?

Health (B)

Word Form Chart

NOUN	VERB	ADJECTIVE	ADVERB
allergy		allergic	
breakout	break out		
	come to		
	cope		
	disagree with		
exhaustion	exhaust	exhausted	
		exhausting	
fatality		fatal	fatally
female		female	
figure			
	get over		
handicap	handicap	handicapped	
insanity		insane	insanely
male		male	
	pass out		
prescription	prescribe	prescribed	
recurrence	recur	recurring	
relief	relieve	relieved	
resumption	resume		
scar	scar	scarred	
sense		sensitive	
sensibility		sensible	sensibly
sex		sexual	sexually
soreness		sore	
tube			
tubing			
vision	visualize	visual	visually
vomit	vomit	vomiting	

Definitions and Examples

1. **scar** [a mark on the skin which is permanent after an injury]

   The accident left a long **scar** on her leg.
   You can recognize him by the **scar** on the right side of his face.

2. **insane** [mentally ill; crazy; mad]

   She is in the hospital for the mentally ill because she is **insane**.
   That murderer must be **insane**; he killed twenty people whom he did not even know.

3. **fatal** [resulting in death]

   There was a **fatal** accident at that intersection last night; two people were killed.
   The disease is always **fatal**; the doctors say that she has only a few months left to live.

4. **fatality** [a death]

   Wars cause many **fatalities**.
   The list of **fatalities** was in the paper on the day after the accident.

5. **come to** [to become conscious]

   He fainted, but he **came to** only a few seconds later.
   When she **came to** after the accident, she was in a hospital room.

6. **get over** [to recover from]

   It will take her at least a month to **get over** this illness.
   The child never **got over** the death of his mother; he is continually sad and troubled.

7. **exhaustion** [a state of extreme tiredness]

   She was suffering from **exhaustion** from her struggle down the mountain after the accident.
   He was so **exhausted** that he could not keep his eyes open.
   Her work has **exhausted** her; she needs to take some days off.

8. **recur** [to occur again after a time period]

   The doctor said that my symptoms may **recur** if I do not get plenty of rest.
   Recurrences of this disease are common, even years later.

9. **allergy** [a negative physical reaction to a food or to something in one's environment]

   Her **allergy** to cats causes her to have trouble breathing when she is near one.
   I do not enjoy picnics because I am **allergic** to grass.

10. **pass out** [to faint; to become unconscious]

> After not eating for a week, he **passed out** from hunger and fell to the floor.
> He cannot become a doctor; he always **passes out** at the sight of blood.

11. **resume** [to return to or begin again after stopping for a time]

> The doctor said that she could **resume** working in about a week.
> You should wait for a month after the operation before **resuming** your normal activities.
> He is looking forward to the **resumption** of his regular activities.

12. **disagree with** (a) [to make one sick]

> Cheese **disagrees with** me, so I never eat it.
> That meal I had last night really **disagreed with** me; I was up sick all night.

> (b) [3-18: to have a different opinion than]

> > My parents **disagree with** me about my plans.

13. **vision** [the ability to see]

> His **vision** is poor so he has to wear glasses all the time.
> People should have their **vision** checked by an eye doctor regularly.
> The teacher used several **visual** aids during his demonstration.

14. **break out** (a) [to develop suddenly]

> An epidemic **broke out** last week; it has already killed thirty people.
> Fighting has **broken out** along the border; this may mean war.
> My skin **breaks out** if I eat too much chocolate.

> (b) [to force one's way out of confinement]

> The prisoners **broke out** of the jail last night.

15. **handicap** (a) [a physical or mental disability]

> His **handicap** did not prevent him from finishing college and getting a good job even though he is confined to a wheelchair.
> A person who is blind is severely visually **handicapped**.
> Mentally **handicapped** children often have great difficulty learning to read.

> (b) [an advantage or disadvantage that is put on a competitor]

> This horse race is a **handicap** race; the fastest horses must carry more weight.

16. **cope** [to deal with difficulty and attempt to succeed anyway]

> She **copes** with her handicap well; it does not keep her from doing her job well.
> When you live in a foreign country, you have to **cope** with many cultural differences.

17. **tube** [a long, thin, flexible pipe, often made of rubber or a rubberlike substance]

> The blood flowed from her arm into the collection bag through a **tube**.
> The seriously ill patient had **tubes** attached to several parts of his body.

18. **prescription** [a written instruction for the preparation and use of a medicine]

> The doctor gave me a **prescription** to take to the drugstore.
> You cannot by that medicine without a **prescription**.
> The doctor **prescribed** three medicines to treat my symptoms.

19. **relief** [the removal or lightening of something painful, tense, or uncomfortable]

> This drug should provide **relief** from the pain caused by your injury.
> His fears about the test were **relieved** by talking to the teacher.
> The **relieved** parents thanked the doctor for saving their baby's life.

20. **sense** (a) [a specialized animal mechanism, such as sight, hearing, smell, taste, or touch]

> His illness has damaged his **sense** of smell.

(b) [a meaning]

> A: What is the **sense** of "cheap" in that sentence?
> B: It means "of poor quality" here.

21. **sensitive** [easily hurt, either physically or emotionally]

> The area around the wound will be **sensitive**, so be careful not to hurt it.
> She is very **sensitive** and cries if someone speaks harshly to her.

22. **sensible** [capable of using one's mind to make practical decisions]

> He is very **sensible**; he will not gamble his money on a foolish scheme.
> It is not **sensible** for you to drop out of school in your senior year.

23. **male** [a man or a boy]

> That is an all-**male** dormitory.
> Mostly **males** suffer from that disease; women rarely get it.

24. **female** [a woman or a girl]

> More **females** than males go into nursing in the United States.
> Male birds are often more brightly colored than **female** ones.

25. **sex** (a) [either of the two divisions of animals called "male" and "female"]

    Under "**sex**" on the form, he checked the box labeled "male."

    (b) [the act between a female and a male that may result in the production of children]

    Many religions consider **sex** outside of marriage to be a sin.

26. **sore** (a) [painful]

    My muscles were **sore** because I had exercised too much.
    She stayed home from school because she had a **sore** throat and a fever.

    (b) [a spot on the body which is damaged and perhaps infected]

    The **sore** on her foot was caused by the poor fit of her new shoes.

27. **vomit** [the act of bringing up food from the stomach and out of the mouth]

    He was **vomiting** because he had food poisoning.
    Her symptoms include a high fever and **vomiting**.

28. **figure** (a) [the bodily shape or form of a person]

    She has a very thin **figure**; she hardly eats enough to live.
    We saw a **figure** in the distance, but we could not see who it was in the dark.

    (b) [2-24: to find an answer, usually using numbers]

    To **figure** the cost of going to the university, you should add the price of tuition, books, and transportation.
    She added the **figures** together to find their sum.

    (c) [5-5: a diagram or illustration used to help explain something]

    The professor told us to look at **figure** number three as he explained the problem.

Introductory Exercises

A. Match each word or phrase with its definition.

_____ 1. the bodily shape or form of a person

_____ 2. a woman or girl

_____ 3. easily hurt

_____ 4. a written instruction for the preparation and use of a medicine

_____ 5. a physical or mental disability

_____ 6. the ability to see

_____ 7. to faint; to become unconscious

_____ 8. a state of extreme tiredness

_____ 9. resulting in death

_____ 10. mentally ill; crazy; mad

_____ 11. to recover from

_____ 12. a negative physical reaction to a food or something in one's environment

_____ 13. to make one sick

_____ 14. to develop with suddenness

_____ 15. a long, thin, flexible pipe, often made of rubber or a rubberlike substance

_____ 16. the removal or lightening of something painful, tense, or uncomfortable

_____ 17. a man or a boy

_____ 18. the act of bringing food up from the stomach and out of the mouth

_____ 19. painful

_____ 20. either of the two divisions of animals called "male" and "female"

_____ 21. to deal with difficulty and attempt to succeed

_____ 22. to return to or begin again after stopping for a time

_____ 23. to become conscious

_____ 24. to occur again after a time period

_____ 25. a mark on the skin which is permanent after an injury

a. allergy
b. break out
c. come to
d. cope
e. disagree with
f. exhaustion
g. fatal
h. female
i. figure
j. get over
k. handicap
l. insane
m. male
n. pass out
o. prescription
p. recur
q. relief
r. resume
s. scar
t. sensitive
u. sex
v. sore
w. tube
x. vision
y. vomit

B.   Answer each question with a word or phrase from the word form chart.

    1. What does someone who is blind have?
    2. What would you feel if you ran ten miles?
    3. What does a person in pain want?
    4. What may remain on your skin after a cut?
    5. What do you have if being near a cat makes you sick?
    6. What do you need to buy certain medicines?
    7. When you give blood, what does the blood flow through after leaving your body?
    8. What does a recovered person hope will not happen?
    9. If you injure your arm, how will your arm feel?
  10. What does a person do after he or she faints?
  11. If you are not male, what are you?
  12. Which sense is related to your eyes?
  13. What may you do if you eat some food that is not fresh?
  14. What may you do if you are in great pain?

Study Exercises

C.   Write **T** if the sentence is true and **F** if it is false.

    _____ **1.** Most people like to have scars.

    _____ **2.** People feel relieved when they get over an illness.

    _____ **3.** A blind person has a vision problem.

    _____ **4.** Anyone can write a prescription for drugs.

    _____ **5.** Insane people make sensible decisions.

    _____ **6.** Your sex is either male or female.

    _____ **7.** An exhausted person needs to sleep.

    _____ **8.** People want to be handicapped.

    _____ **9.** People recover from fatal accidents.

    _____ **10.** A person who is allergic to a certain food should not eat that food.

    _____ **11.** Health officials try to avoid breakouts of epidemics.

    _____ **12.** A person cannot come to after he or she passes out.

    _____ **13.** If you are allergic to a food, it disagrees with you.

D. Complete each analogy with a word or phrase from the word form chart.

1. body : sick :: mind : _____

2. ears : hearing :: eyes : _____

3. left : right :: male : _____

4. faint : pass out :: wake up : _____

5. stain : clothing :: _____ : skin

6. food : hunger :: sleep : _____

7. red : color :: male : _____

E. In each blank, write the most appropriate two- or three-word verb from the following list.

break down	come out with	get away with	pass on
break in	come to	get by with	pass out
break into		get on with	
break up		get over	
break out			

1. The little boy promised to _____ my message to his mother.

2. Disease can _____ in a community when conditions are not sanitary.

3. The scientist returned from his vacation early because he was in a hurry to _____ his research.

4. The patient took a long time to _____ after his operation. The doctors waited for him to open his eyes.

5. I _____ my cold in only three days; usually a cold lasts longer than that.

6. It is very sad when a married couple _____ .

7. It was so hot and he was so exhausted that he _____ .

8. The new product that our company _____ last year is selling very well.

9. These shoes are not _____ yet; look at this sore on my foot.

10. The teacher said that our reports should be at least ten pages long. I hope I can _____ this one; it's only eight pages.

F.   In each blank, write the most appropriate word or phrase from the word form chart.

Until very recently, polio epidemics were a common occurrence in the United States, especially during the summer months. Each year, as the warm weather approached, the people waited with fear for the disease to (1) _____ . Polio caused great fear because it was (2) _____ for many of its victims. Other victims (3) _____ the disease but were left (4) _____ . Many survivors were never able to walk again.

Until 1955 there was no effective cure or method to prevent polio. Young and old, male and (5) _____ , everyone was a possible future victim. Doctors found it very difficult to (6) _____ with a disease for which they had no effective drugs to (7) _____ . Each summer they could only caution the people to avoid public swimming pools and other public gatherings, where it was believed people caught the disease. But the fears of the medical world and the public were calmed in 1955 with the announcement from Dr. Jonas Salk that his research team had found a way to prevent polio. A general feeling of (8) _____ was apparent all over the country.

Follow-up

G.   Dictation: Write the sentences that your teacher reads aloud.

1. _____
2. _____
3. _____
4. _____
5. _____

H.   Answer the following questions.

1. Do you have any allergies? Explain.
2. Have you ever passed out? If so, what were the circumstances?
3. How long does it usually take you to get over a cold?
4. Name some medicines that are available only by prescription in your country.
5. Do you have any scars? If so, what are they the result of?

6. Does the government in your country do anything to help handicapped people? Explain.
7. What do you usually do to get relief from a headache?
8. Do you have any problems with your vision? Explain.
9. Have any epidemics broken out in your country recently? Explain.
10. What happens to people who are insane?
11. What should you do if your throat is sore? Your leg?

I.   Choose one disease, and describe what usually happens to a person who has it.

Media (B)

Word Form Chart

NOUN	VERB	ADJECTIVE	ADVERB
ambiguity		ambiguous	ambiguously
	bring out		
	catch on		
chronology		chronological	chronologically
comprehension	comprehend	comprehensible	comprehensibly
consistency		consistent	consistently
format	format		
gap			
	get across		
gossip	gossip	gossipy	
		gossiping	
heading	head		
head			
impression	impress	impressive	impressively
interruption	interrupt	interrupted	
	leave out		
	look up		
nonsense		nonsensical	nonsensically
	pass out		
pertinence	pertain	pertinent	pertinently
		impertinent	impertinently
reference	refer		
reflection	reflect	reflecting	
		reflected	
regard	regard		regardless
irrelevance		irrelevant	irrelevantly
relevance		relevant	relevantly
revision	revise	revised	
supposition	suppose	supposed	supposedly
validity		valid	validly
		invalid	invalidly

Definitions and Examples

1. **leave out** {separable} [to not include]

   > The editor decided to **leave out** many of the details because the article was too long.

   > A: Should I write the names of the victims in my story?
   > B: No. **Leave** them **out**.

2. **catch on** [to become popular]

   > That new book has really **caught on**; everyone is reading it.
   > Some fashions **catch on** quickly; others take some time to become popular.

3. **ambiguous** [having more than one meaning; confusing]

   > You need to rewrite this sentence because it is **ambiguous**; the readers will not understand it.
   > I am not sure what he meant because his words were **ambiguous**.

4. **chronological** [organized according to time order]

   > The easiest way to tell a story is in **chronological** order.
   > The police are not yet certain about the **chronology** of the crime.

5. **revise** [to change something, often in order to make it better]

   > I have to **revise** my paper before I hand it in tomorrow.
   > If it rains tomorrow, we will have to **revise** our plans.

6. **pass out** {separable} (a) [to distribute; to hand out]

   > My boss **passes out** our assignments for the day each morning.
   > An old man was giving people free papers today; he was **passing** them **out** in front of the church.

   > (b) [5-23: to faint; to lose consciousness]

   > > She **passed out** from the heat and fell to the floor.

7. **gossip** [to talk about other people's personal affairs]

   > My mother told me not to **gossip**.
   > Everyone **gossips** about him because they do not approve of the things he does.
   > That is not official information; it is only **gossip**.

8. **valid** (a) [supported by truth or generally accepted authority]

Your argument against the project is not **valid**; many of your facts are wrong.

He will not reach an accurate conclusion because some of his initial assumptions are not **valid**.

(b) [having legal force]

That driver's license is not **valid** because it is too old.

9. **nonsense** (a) [words or language having no meaning]

The child spoke, but we could not understand his **nonsense**.

(b) [an action or situation which goes against good sense]

That plan to use balloons for transportation within the city is **nonsensical**; it will never work.

10. **bring out** (a) [to present to the public]

That company is **bringing out** several new products this year.
That magazine was first **brought out** last year.

(b) [to make apparent]

This article really **brings out** several important issues in his speech.

11. **comprehend** [to understand]

She did not **comprehend** most of what the teacher said and decided to go to the beginning class.
He reads rapidly, but his **comprehension** is not good.
I do not find his ideas to be **comprehensible**.

12. **head** (a) [to come at the beginning]

The title **headed** the article.
The **heading** of a business letter includes the date and the address of the person to whom you are sending the letter.

(b) [the leader]

The **head** of the club gave the first speech.

(c) [assumed: the part of the body containing the brain and the mouth]

He put his hat on his **head**.

13. **suppose** [to assume; to guess; to think probable]

I **suppose** that I should continue to revise this paper until it seems clear.
The **supposed** kidnapper helped the police to find the real kidnappers and their victim.
In order to do this problem, several **suppositions** are necessary.

14. **consistent** [having steady continuity; free from irregularity]

> Her work is very **consistent**; it is always good.
> He was fired because he was **consistently** late to work.

15. **consistency** [the degree of firmness or thickness]

> This food has the **consistency** of a thick soup.

16. **format** [the shape, size, or general plan of organization or arrangement]

> His job at the newspaper is to decide the **format** of each page of the sports section.
> The **format** of this television program must include advertisements four times.

17. **gap** (a) [a separation in space]

> He has a **gap** between his two front teeth.
> We passed through the mountain **gap**.

(b) [a break in continuity]

> That story has too many **gaps** in it to make sense.
> My grandmother has many **gaps** in her memory now; she has forgotten entire years of her life.

18. **relevant** [relating to the topic under consideration]

> The editor removed that description because he thought that it was not **relevant**.
> The professor gave me a bad grade; he said that my answer was interesting, but not **relevant** to the question.
> The judge will not permit **irrelevant** questions to be asked during the trial.

19. **get across** {separable} [to communicate effectively]

> I have to revise this article because it does not **get across** my main ideas well.
> The taxi driver did not understand English, and I could not **get across** the name of the place where I wanted to go.
> That professor understands that explanation well, but he is having trouble **getting** it **across** to his students.

20. **impress** [to affect; to influence]

> The boss was **impressed** by the hard-working young woman.
> He was not polite to his girlfriend's parents and made a very bad **impression**.
> The contents of the newspaper article **impressed** the readers so much that many of them wrote to the newspaper.

21. **interrupt** [to break the continuity of]

> My phone call was **interrupted** by the arrival of a guest.
> He **interrupted** his work to eat lunch.
> I am bothered by **interruptions** when I am studying.

22. **refer (to)** (a) [to think of or classify within a category or group]

> The word "alcoholic" **refers to** a person who cannot control his or her use of alcohol.
> That point in the president's speech **referred to** an event that occurred last year.

   (b) [to send or direct for treatment or advice]

> His family doctor **referred** him **to** a specialist to treat his skin problem.

   (c) [to direct attention, usually by clear and specific mention]

> Do not **refer to** the party when you are talking to my mother. It is a surprise.

   (d) [to consult; to look at briefly]

> The teacher said that we could **refer to** our notes during our speeches.
> I will have to **refer to** a dictionary to understand these words.
> A dictionary is a type of **reference** book.
> When you **refer to** certain sources in order to write a paper, you must list your **references** at the end of the paper.

23. **look up** {separable} (a) [to search for in a reference book]

> I had to **look up** many words in order to understand that article in French.
> If you do not know his number, **look** it **up** in the telephone book.

   (b) {informal} [to improve in condition]

> Her business should be **looking up** soon; the type of shoes she makes are becoming quite popular.
> Cheer up, my friend, your luck will **look up** before long.

24. **pertinent** [relevant to the topic under consideration]

> The police want to know all the information that is **pertinent** to the crime.
> I think this article **pertains** to the problem we are researching.

25. **impertinent** [rude; not within the boundaries of good taste]

> My parents did not like him because he made some **impertinent** comments to them.

26. **reflect** (a) [to turn, throw, or bend back something from a surface]

> A mirror **reflects** light.
> She looked in the mirror and saw her **reflection**.
> The sky and the brightly colored trees were **reflected** in the calm surface of the lake.

(b) [to show]

> Her poor grades **reflect** her lack of interest in school.
> The attitude of the author of the article **reflects** the general attitude of the public.

(c) [to think quietly and calmly]

> You should **reflect** on this problem before you make a decision.
> After **reflecting** on it, I have decided to quit my job.
> This dilemma requires **reflection**.

27. **regard** (a) [to consider]

> I **regard** him as my best friend.

(b) [the worth or estimation in which something is held]

> I have a high **regard** for that professor and her work.
> He is highly **regarded** as a doctor.

28. **as regards** [concerning]

> **As regards** her health, she should get more exercise.

29. **regardless** [despite everything]

> They had many problems; they continued with their plans **regardless**.

30. **regarding** [concerning]

> I have no advice for you **regarding** that problem.

Introductory Exercises

A.   Match each word or phrase with its definition.

_____	**1.** to show	**a.** ambiguous
_____	**2.** to search for in a reference book	**b.** bring out
_____	**3.** to consult; to look at briefly	**c.** catch on
_____	**4.** to effectively communicate	**d.** chronological
_____	**5.** the shape, size, or general plan of organization or arrangement	**e.** comprehend
_____	**6.** to assume; to guess; to think probable	**f.** consistent
_____	**7.** to present to the public	**g.** format
_____	**8.** to talk about other people's personal affairs	**h.** gap
_____	**9.** organized according to time order	**i.** get across
_____	**10.** to not include	**j.** gossip
_____	**11.** having more than one meaning; confusing	**k.** head
_____	**12.** to distribute; to hand out	**l.** impress
_____	**13.** words or language having no meaning	**m.** interrupt
_____	**14.** to come at the beginning	**n.** leave out
_____	**15.** having steady continuity; free from irregularity	**o.** look up
_____	**16.** to break the continuity of	**p.** nonsense
_____	**17.** to consider	**q.** pass out
_____	**18.** to affect; to influence	**r.** pertinent
_____	**19.** a separation in space	**s.** refer
_____	**20.** to become popular	**t.** reflect
_____	**21.** supported by truth or generally accepted authority	**u.** regard
_____	**22.** to change something often in order to make it better	**v.** relevant
_____	**23.** to understand	**w.** revise
		x. suppose
		y. valid

B.   Answer each question with a word from the word form chart.

1. In what order do people usually tell stories?
2. What does a writer do to his work to make it better?
3. What are you doing if you speak while another person is speaking?
4. What does an editor do to a part of a story that he does not want to include?

5. What does a teacher do with homework papers in class?
6. What can you do if you are reading something and don't know the meaning of a word?
7. What do you see when you look in the mirror?
8. What kind of a book is a dictionary?
9. What is a person that talks a lot about other people's private activities?
10. What does a publishing company do with books?
11. What kind of a driver's license should you have to legally drive?

Study Exercises

C. Write **T** if the sentence is true and **F** if it is false.

_____ 1. An ambiguous sentence is easy to understand.

_____ 2. A fact which is relevant to a topic pertains to that topic.

_____ 3. An impertinent person is not polite.

_____ 4. It is easy to understand something that is nonsense.

_____ 5. The heading of an article comes at the beginning.

_____ 6. A speaker who gets across his meaning well is easy to understand.

_____ 7. A child who is consistently bad is bad most of the time.

_____ 8. Interrupting a speaker is polite.

_____ 9. People look up information in reference books.

_____ 10. If you hold a person in high regard, you respect him or her.

_____ 11. If, when you tell a story, you leave out important events, there will be gaps in the story.

_____ 12. Most people enjoy it when others gossip about them.

_____ 13. All magazines have the same format.

_____ 14. Your listening comprehension is how well you understand when you listen to people speak.

D. Complete the analogies with a word or phrase from the word form chart.

1. clothing : pattern :: newspaper : _____
2. building : repair :: article : _____
3. book : publish :: car _____
4. true : valid :: false : _____
5. white : black :: include : _____
6. book : title :: article : _____
7. see : dark :: comprehend : _____

E. Match each two- or three-word verb with its definition. You may use some letters more than once.

___ **1.** bring about	**a.** to cause
___ **2.** bring off	**b.** to raise
___ **3.** bring on	**c.** to carry out to a successful conclusion
___ **4.** bring out	**d.** to present to the public
___ **5.** bring up	**e.** to happen
___ **6.** catch on	**f.** to reach the level of others who have done more than you have
___ **7.** catch up	**g.** to become popular
___ **8.** come about	**h.** to understand
___ **9.** come along	**i.** to be published
___ **10.** come down with	**j.** to bring to the public attention
___ **11.** come out with	**k.** to become sick with
___ **12.** come to	**l.** to become conscious
___ **13.** get across	**m.** to accompany
___ **14.** get away with	**n.** to continue
___ **15.** get on with	**o.** to escape without punishment for
___ **16.** get over	**p.** to communicate effectively
	q. to survive
	r. to recover from

F. In each blank, write the most appropriate word or phrase from the word form chart.

Many students of English as a second language make the mistake of (1) _____ too many words in their dictionaries as they read. To learn to read and (2) _____ well in English, a student should have a system for deciding when to consult a (3) _____ book for the meanings of words that he does not know. A student should not (4) _____ his reading too often or his comprehension will not be good. He should understand that not all the words that a writer uses are equally (5) _____ to the writer's main ideas. Therefore, a reader need not look up unknown words that are obviously (6) _____ to the main topics of the reading. A student can also use the (7) _____ of a reading to help him know which unknown words to look up. For example, words that appear in the (8) _____ of an article are usually central to the main points of the article. Unimportant words are often (9) _____ of headings, so all of the words that appear are likely to be important. In short, students should develop a system for deciding when they must (10) _____ to a dictionary. If they consistently look up all the unknown words in every article that they read, they will spend more time reading their dictionary than reading the articles which they have been assigned.

Follow-up

G. Dictation: Write the sentences that your teacher reads aloud.

1. _____
2. _____
3. _____
4. _____
5. _____

H. Answer the following questions.

1. What must you do to be polite if you need to interrupt someone in English?
2. What are some of the format characteristics in a typical newspaper in your country?
3. Name something that has recently caught on in your country.
4. Under what circumstances do you look up a word in English?
5. Do people in your country pass out any kind of literature on the streets? What kind?
6. Do different newspapers in your country reflect different viewpoints? Give some examples.
7. What is the most impressive place in your country?
8. What do you think are the worst gaps in your knowledge of English?
9. What is in the heading of a business letter in your country?

I. Describe what makes a person an effective public speaker. What must he or she do to be effective? How must he or she speak?

Crime (B)

Word Form Chart

NOUN	VERB	ADJECTIVE	ADVERB
admission	admit	admitted	
article			
		capital	
case			
charge	charge		
	clear out		
convict	convict	convicted	
conviction			
cruelty		cruel	cruelly
deception	deceive		
detection	detect		
detective			
enforcement		enforceable	
enforceability	enforce		
enforcer			
execution	execute		
executioner			
frustration	frustrate	frustrating	
		frustrated	
	get around		
	hand over		
holdup	hold up		
juvenile		juvenile	
motive	motivate	motivating	
motivation		motivated	
observation	observe	observed	
panic	panic	panicky	
pistol			
prohibition	prohibit	prohibited	
testimony	testify		

NOUN	VERB	ADJECTIVE	ADVERB
thief			
thievery		thieving	
theft			
verdict			

Definitions and Examples

1. **convict** (a) [to find someone guilty in a court]

    He was **convicted** of robbing the bank and was sent to prison.
    The jury **convicted** her of murder.
    I read about that murderer's **conviction** in the paper.

    (b) [a person who is serving a prison sentence]

    The **convicts** have jobs inside the prisons.
    Three **convicts** escaped from the jail last night.

2. **conviction** [a strong belief]

    He has strong **convictions** about his job; he will not change his mind.
    She will not go against her **convictions**.

3. **juvenile** (a) [a young person]

    He will not be sent to jail because he is a **juvenile**.
    In some cities there is a lot of crime among **juveniles**.

    (b) [characteristic of or suitable for young people]

    You can find that book in the **juvenile** section of the library.
    She studies **juvenile** psychology.

4. **observe** (a) [to watch carefully in order to learn]

    You should **observe** the demonstration carefully.
    The police **observed** the man break into the store.

    (b) [to comment]

    He **observed** that there would be no class tomorrow.
    She made the **observation** that it was raining.

    (c) [to celebrate]

    Not everyone **observes** New Year's Day on January 1.
    He is **observing** his country's holidays although he is living in the United
       States this year.

5. **pistol** [a small handgun]

    The robber used a **pistol** during the robbery.
    She was murdered by a man with a **pistol**.

6. **panic** [to feel sudden, very strong fear, often among a group of people]

   Everyone **panicked** and ran away when they saw the pistol in the man's hand.
   The bank teller did not **panic** during the robbery; she quietly pushed the
   alarm button to call the police.

7. **prohibit** [to not permit]

   The convicts were **prohibited** from smoking in their cells.
   My parents **prohibited** me from getting a driver's license until I was
   eighteen.

8. **cruel** [causing pain and unhappiness]

   The kidnappers were **cruel** to their victim and did not give him food and
   water.
   Cruelty to animals is a crime in many countries.

9. **article** (a) [a thing]

   The police asked for descriptions of the stolen **articles**.
   Only one **article** was of great value: a diamond ring.

   (b) [2-17: a piece of writing in a newspaper or magazine]

   The most important **articles** in a newspaper are usually on the
   first page.

10. **hand over** {separable} [to give]

    The criminal **handed** his pistol **over** to the policeman who had captured him.
    The boss **hands** many of his responsibilities **over** to his assistant.

11. **hold up** {separable} [to rob with a weapon]

    Three men **held up** that bank yesterday.
    I was **held up** in the park last night by a man with a pistol.
    The man who **held** me **up** said he needed money.

    (b) [to delay; to slow]

    Traffic was **held up** by an accident this morning.
    My flight should have arrived already, but the fog **held** it **up**.

12. **deceive** [to cause to accept as true or valid something that is false]

    He **deceived** his mother by telling her that the toy he had stolen was a
    gift from a friend.
    They knew that she had been lying when they discovered her **deception**.

13. **admit** (a) [to say that something is true and valid]

    The criminal **admitted** that he had robbed the bank.
    He refuses to **admit** that he is addicted to drugs.
    Her **admission** of guilt was used as evidence against her in court.

    (b) [3-3: to permit to enter]

    He was **admitted** to a good university.

14. **case** (a) [an action in a court of law]

> His **case** will come to trial next week.
> The media is watching this **case** closely because the public is very interested in it.

(b) [an occurrence of disease or injury]

> He has a bad **case** of the measles.
> Her broken back is the most serious **case** the doctor is treating right now.

(c) [a situation requiring investigation or action, for example by the police]

> The police are looking into three **cases** of murder this week.
> Two more policemen have been assigned to that **case**.

(d) [a condition]

> In any **case**, you should study hard for the final exam.

(e) [an argument in favor of something]

> The police have a good **case** against the accused man.
> You have a **case** for what you want to do, but I do not agree with you.

15. **verdict** [the decision on a case in court]

> It took the jury three days to reach a **verdict** of innocent.
> The **verdict** for that case is still uncertain.

16. **thief** {plural: thieves} [a person who steals]

> The **thieves** entered the house through an open window.
> The family was saddened by the **theft** of many of their possessions.
> That store has lost a lot of money because of **thievery** by its employees.

17. **motive** [something that causes a person to act]

> The police have not yet figured out the **motive** behind the murders.
> Students with strong **motivation** to learn usually study a lot and learn quickly.
> Employers want to have well-**motivated** employees who will work hard.

18. **execute** (a) [to put to death according to a legal sentence]

> The murderer was **executed** in the electric chair.
> The countries which permit **executions** of criminals use various methods to carry out the death sentence.

(b) [to carry out]

> The soldiers **executed** their officer's orders.
> The computer will **execute** whatever commands you enter into it.

19. **detect** [to discover or determine the existence, presence, or fact of]

> It is difficult to **detect** the presence of some defects in the merchandise.
> The police **detectives** are investigating the crime.
> Crime **detection** has become a science with the introduction of new techniques and instruments for finding clues.

20. **get around** [to avoid (an obstacle)]

The thieves **got around** the police cars and escaped.
She always **gets around** the rules and does things her way.
People often try to **get around** paying their taxes.

21. **testimony** [evidence given by a person]

Her **testimony** included everything that she had seen at the scene of the crime.
The witnesses of the robbery were asked to **testify** in court.
She **testified** to the guilt of the accused man.

22. **frustrate** [to cause feelings of discouragement]

The lack of evidence in this case is **frustrating** the police detectives.
The **frustrated** child began to cry when he could not reach the candy.
Frustration with living in poverty causes some people to turn to crime.

23. **charge (with)** (a) [to accuse formally (of)]

They **charged** the man whom they had arrested with robbery and murder.
He was convicted on the murder **charge** and sentenced to death.

(b) [2-9: to make someone pay]

I go to that store because they **charge** low prices.

24. **clear out** {informal} (a) [to leave]

The thieves **cleared out** before the police arrived.
We should **clear out** now; the store is closing in two minutes.

(b) {separable} [to remove the contents of a three-dimensional space]

We need to **clear** all that junk **out** of the garage.
The police **cleared out** the building so that no one would get hurt.

25. **capital** (a) [punishable by death]

People who are convicted of **capital** crimes may be executed. Murder is a
capital offense in many countries.

(b) [2-11: the city where the government of a country or state is located]

Washington, D.C., is the **capital** of the United States.

(c) [5-4: large (used only to describe letters in writing)]

Use a **capital** letter to begin the first word in a sentence.

(d) [5-6: money and possessions]

You need **capital** to start a business.

26. **enforce** [to use greater strength or power to make sure that something is done]

The police **enforce** the laws.
That teacher never **enforces** her rules strictly.
She wants a career in law **enforcement**.
Such a low speed limit on the road will be **unenforceable**.

Introductory Exercises

A. Match each word or phrase with its definition.

____ **1.** a young person		**a.** admit
____ **2.** to use power in making sure something is carried out		**b.** article
		c. capital
____ **3.** a small handgun		**d.** case
____ **4.** causing pain and unhappiness		**e.** charge
		f. clear out
____ **5.** to rob with a weapon		**g.** convict
____ **6.** an action in a court of law		**h.** cruel
____ **7.** a person who steals		**i.** deceive
		j. detect
____ **8.** to discover or determine the existence, presence, or fact of		**k.** enforce
		l. execute
____ **9.** to cause feelings of discouragement		**m.** frustrate
____ **10.** punishable by death		**n.** get around
		o. hand over
____ **11.** to leave		**p.** hold up
____ **12.** evidence given by a person		**q.** juvenile
		r. motive
____ **13.** to accuse formally		**s.** observe
____ **14.** to avoid (an obstacle)		**t.** panic
		u. pistol
____ **15.** to put to death according to a legal sentence		**v.** prohibit
		w. testimony
____ **16.** something that causes a person to act		**x.** thief
____ **17.** the decision on a case in court		**y.** verdict

____ **18.** to say that something is true and valid

____ **19.** to cause to accept as true or valid something that is false

____ **20.** to give

____ **21.** a thing

____ **22.** to not permit

____ **23.** a sudden, unreasonable fear, often among a group of people

____ **24.** to watch carefully in order to learn

____ **25.** to find someone guilty in a court

B. Answer each question with a word from the word form chart.

1. What sometimes happens to a person convicted of murder?
2. If you are not an adult, what are you?
3. How do you feel if you cannot do something that you want to do?
4. Who investigates crimes?

5. What is a typical holdup weapon?
6. What do witnesses to a crime give at a trial?
7. What does the jury decide at a trial?
8. What kind of punishment is execution?
9. What is a lie an example of?
10. Who do you find in prison?
11. What do the police do to suspected criminals?
12. Who steals things?

Study Exercises

C. Write **T** if the sentence is true and **F** if it is false.

_____ 1. People should do things that are prohibited.

_____ 2. People try to get around things that they like.

_____ 3. Many convicts are guilty of crimes.

_____ 4. A person who confesses is admitting his or her guilt.

_____ 5. Criminals often deceive people.

_____ 6. Someone's motivation explains his or her actions.

_____ 7. A juvenile is an old person.

_____ 8. A pistol may be used during a holdup.

_____ 9. A person's testimony should be a deception.

_____ 10. People do not like to be frustrated.

_____ 11. A cruel person hurts other people.

_____ 12. The police want to charge innocent people.

D. Complete each analogy with a word from the word form chart.

1. doctor : diagnose :: _____ : investigate

2. color : red :: _____ : guilty

3. cook : eat :: _____ : convict

4. color : green :: sentence : _____

5. black : white :: deny : _____

6. observation : watching :: robbery : _____

7. yes : no :: permit : _____

8. hunger : eat :: _____ : act

9. doctor : treatment :: witness : _____

E. Match each two-word verb with its definition. You may use a letter more than once.

_____ **1.** clear out

_____ **2.** clear up

_____ **3.** hand down

_____ **4.** hand out

_____ **5.** hand over

_____ **6.** hold up

a. to give
b. to give to a younger relative
c. to become clear
d. to leave
e. to distribute
f. to find the solution to
g. to clear the inside of a three-dimensional space
h. to rob with a gun

F. In each blank, write the most appropriate word or phrase from the word form chart.

Yesterday, there was a (1) _____ at the First National Bank on Main Street. Three men carrying (2) _____ entered the bank at 2:00 P.M. and demanded that the tellers (3) _____ all the money in their drawers. One of the tellers pressed a silent alarm button during the robbery, but the thieves had (4) _____ by the time that the police arrived. Fortunately, no one (5) _____ during the robbery, and no one was hurt.

Police (6) _____ questioned the witnesses, who said that one of the three robbers was only a (7) _____ , perhaps sixteen years old. All of the witnesses agreed to (8) _____ in court when the three are arrested and (9) _____ with armed robbery. The police are confident that the (10) _____ of the witnesses will lead to the (11) _____ of the robbers.

Follow-up

G. Dictation: Write the sentences that your teacher reads aloud.

1. _____

2. _____

3. _____

4. _____

5. _____

H.   Answer the following questions.

1. Do most criminals in your country admit their guilt when they are caught? Explain.
2. What are the most commonly stolen articles in your country? Explain.
3. Can a person in your country be held in jail without first being charged with a crime? Explain.
4. Explain some crime detection methods used in your country.
5. What makes you frustrated?
6. Have you ever witnessed a holdup? Explain.
7. What motivates you to study English?
8. Name something that is prohibited in your country.
9. Have you ever really panicked? When? Explain.
10. Is crime a problem among juveniles in your country? Explain.

I.   Explain the possible sentences in a murder case in your country. Is capital punishment used?

Answer Key

Unit 1

C. 1. F 2. T 3. T 4. F 5. F 6. F 7. T 8. T 9. F 10. T 11. T 12. F
13. F 14. F

D. 1. mayor 2. visa 3. reform 4. sympathize 5. run for 6. step aside

E. 1. at least two 2. Their approaches to issues are not viewed sympathetically by the majority of the voters. 3. Republican 4. gradually, because the two major parties are quite similar

Unit 2

C. 1. T 2. F 3. T 4. T 5. F 6. T 7. F 8. T 9. T 10. T 11. T 12. T
13. T 14. F

D. 1. for 2. down 3. with 4. on 5. against 6. up 7. to 8. aside
9. over 10. up 11. up 12. under

E. 1. wound 2. depress 3. cease 4. lately 5. ineffective 6. cheery
7. anticipated 8. unbearable

F. 1. mood 2. wound 3. symptom 4. lately 5. temperature 6. effective

G. 1. mood 2. anticipate 3. confident 4. cheery 5. bear up under 6. treat
7. depressed 8. effective 9. cheer up 10. drugs.

Unit 3

C. 1. F 2. T 3. F 4. T 5. F 6. F 7. T 8. T 9. T 10. F 11. T 12. F
13. F 14. F 15. T

D. 1. j 2. f 3. a 4. o 5. g 6. b 7. p 8. c 9. d 10. m 11. h
12. e 13. n 14. i

E. 1. swamp 2. clear up/let up/blow over 3. vapor 4. gloomy
5. indication 6. vast 7. optimum/optimal 8. wood(s) 9. uneasy

F. 1. vegetation 2. gloomy 3. moist 4. vapor 5. current 6. channel
7. phenomena 8. uneasiness

Unit 4

C. 1. F 2. T 3. T 4. T 5. F 6. F 7. F 8. F 9. T 10. T 11. T 12. F
13. T 14. T

D. 1. f 2. a 3. k 4. c 5. h 6. b 7. d 8. g 9. j

E. 1. k 2. j 3. l 4. e 5. b 6. h 7. f 8. c 9. a 10. d 11. g

F. 1. glances 2. focuses on 3. put across/written up 4. written up/put
across 5. reaction 6. omits 7. censorship 8. interpretation 9. pass on/put
across/focus on 10. circulation

Unit 5

C. 1. F 2. T 2. T 3. T 4. T 5. F 6. F 7. F 8. F 9. T 10. T 11. T 12. F

D. 1. c, going over 2. b, handed out 3. c, write up 4. a, put across 5. a, fallen
behind 6. b, catch up 7. c, drop out of 8. c, turned down

E. 1. fulfill 2. submit 3. means 4. competent 5. ratio 6. drop out of
7. foundation 8. prefer

Unit 6

C. 1. T 2. F 3. T 4. F 5. F 6. T 7. F 8. T 9. F 10. F 11. F 12. T
13. F 14. T 15. T

D. 1. b, c, d, h, j, l 2. a, d, g, i k 3. e, f, i

E. 1. f 2. d 3. a 4. i 5. b 6. e 7. j

F. 1. fix up 2. capital 3. plumber 4. rusty 5. sewer 6. access 7. attic
8. cleaned out 9. installation 10. insulated 11. shortage

Unit 7

C. 1. F 2. F 3. T 4. F 5. T 6. F 7. T 8. T 9. F 10. F 11. T 12. F
13. T 14. T

D. 1. pump 2. acre 3. calf 4. harvest 5. nurse 6. veterinarian 7. yield
8. earth 9. persist 10. scatter

E. 1. f 2. i 3. n 4. a 5. j 6. l 7. b 8. e 9. c 10. g 11. d 12. m

F. 1. failed to 2. got by/carried on/persisted 3. look back on 4. persistence
5. hardships 6. carry on 7. looking after 8. earth 9. harvest 10. work out

Unit 8

C. 1. T 2. T 3. F 4. T 5. F 6. F 7. F 8. T 9. T 10. F 11. T 12. F
13. F 14. F 15. T 16. T

D. 1. e 2. h 3. b 4. j 5. a 6. d 7. c 8. i

E. 1. d 2. o 3. a 4. b 5. j 6. f 7. n 8. h 9. c 10. i 11. e 12. m
13. k 14. l

F. 1. b 2. c 3. c 4. c 5. a 6. a

G. 1. work out 2. do it over 3. carry out 4. get on with/carry on with 5. fill
out 6. filling in for 7. get on with/carry on with 8. worked out 9. look
back on

Unit 9

C. **1.** T **2.** T **3.** F **4.** F **5.** T **6.** F **7.** T **8.** T **9.** F **10.** T **11.** T **12.** T
13. F

D. **1.** blow up **2.** retreat **3.** outcome **4.** discipline **5.** troop **6.** victory
7. enlist **8.** give away **9.** hero/victor/heroine/conqueror

E. **1.** d **2.** a **3.** d **4.** b **5.** b **6.** a **7.** c **8.** a **9.** c

F. **1.** rebels' **2.** victory **3.** discipline **4.** troops **5.** enlisted **6.** flee/give up
7. arms **8.** lay in **9.** struggle/campaign/campaign/resistance/rebellion
10. campaign/struggle **11.** die down **12.** give up

Unit 10

C. **1.** F **2.** T **3.** T **4.** T **5.** T **6.** F **7.** T **8.** T **9.** F **10.** T **11.** T
12. F **13.** F

D. **1.** escort **2.** kidnap **3.** suspect **4.** wealth **5.** evidence **6.** ransom
7. threaten

E. **1.** break into **2.** tied up **3.** look into/check up on **4.** clear up; checking up
on/looking into **5.** gave up

F. **1.** sentenced **2.** broke into **3.** release **4.** ransom **5.** accused
6. evidence **7.** inquiry **8.** trial **9.** involved **10.** sentenced

Unit 11

C. **1.** F **2.** F **3.** T **4.** T **5.** F **6.** T **7.** T **8.** F **9.** T **10.** F **11.** T **12.** T
13. F **14.** F **15.** F **16.** T

D. Errors: **1.** ten calories **2.** four plastic tomatoes **3.** cut down the meat
4. filled up on water **5.** cut out the remaining vegetables **6.** put the potatoes
away **7.** starving

E. **1.** People have become more health conscious **2.** eating fewer garbage foods,
eating more nutritious snacks, eating less beef and more vegetables **3.** taking
more time, eating in quiet restaurants with more leisurely atmospheres, at
home no phone or TV interruptions **4.** fewer fattening ingredients,
substituting vegetable oil for butter **5.** anorexia **6.** lose as much as 50% of
their body weight **7.** educating the public about proper ways to exercise and
diet and places to go for medical help

Unit 12

C. **1.** F **2.** T **3.** T **4.** T **5.** T **6.** T **7.** T **8.** F **9.** T **10.** T **11.** T **12.** F
13. T **14.** T **15.** T

D. **1.** snow **2.** tree **3.** baby **4.** invisible **5.** jury **6.** area **7.** movies **8.** ray
9. philosophy **10.** water

E. **1.** contract **2.** battery **3.** conductor/conduct **4.** work out **5.** think up
6. statistician **7.** area

F. **1.** light and heat **2.** They use some of the visible radiation to produce
food. **3.** no **4.** major disturbances of the sun's outer regions **5.** They have a
fairly well-defined frequency of occurrence. **6.** in all living things; in
diamonds; in oil

Unit 13

C.   **1.** F   **2.** T   **3.** T   **4.** F   **5.** F   **6.** T   **7.** F   **8.** T   **9.** F   **10.** T   **11.** F   **12.** T

D.   **1.** rage   **2.** tragedy   **3.** rehearse   **4.** episode   **5.** call off   **6.** tear   **7.** die away   **8.** frame   **9.** gallery   **10.** make up

E.   **1.** c   **2.** b   **3.** e   **4.** g   **5.** j   **6.** h   **7.** i   **9.** f   **10.** d

F.   **1.** shocked   **2.** tragic   **3.** portable   **4.** make up   **5.** versatile   **6.** rehearsing   **7.** tore up   **8.** called off   **9.** role   **10.** opportunity; episode

Unit 14

C.   **1.** F   **2.** T   **3.** T   **4.** F   **5.** F   **6.** T   **7.** F   **8.** T   **9.** T   **10.** T   **11.** T   **12.** F   **13.** F   **14.** F

D.   **1.** controversy   **2.** chop down   **3.** fragile   **4.** ecologist   **5.** cut off   **6.** application

E.   **1.** the swamp   **2.** wealth   **3.** agency   **4.** an expert   **5.** tractor   **6.** rock   **7.** a compensation   **8.** a dormitory

F.   **1.** F   **2.** F   **3.** T   **4.** F   **5.** F   **6.** T

Unit 15

C.   **1.** F   **2.** T   **3.** T   **4.** F   **5.** T   **6.** F   **7.** F   **8.** T   **9.** T   **10.** T   **11.** F   **12.** T   **13.** T   **14.** F

D.   **1.** stocking   **2.** let down   **3.** try on   **4.** fade   **5.** ink   **6.** costume   **7.** nude

E.   **1.** pick out   **2.** worn off   **3.** tried...on   **4.** dressed up   **5.** takes...off   **6.** let out   **7.** wear out   **8.** go with   **9.** took in   **10.** showing off   **11.** let down

F.   **1.** utility   **2.** wears out   **3.** showing off   **4.** textiles   **5.** synthetic   **6.** dressed up   **7.** go with   **8.** have on

Unit 16

C.   **1.** T   **2.** F   **3.** F   **4.** F   **5.** T   **6.** F   **7.** T   **8.** F   **9.** F   **10.** T   **11.** T   **12.** T   **13.** T   **14.** T   **15.** T   **16.** T   **17.** T

D.   **1.** expert   **2.** focus   **3.** of water   **4.** luxury   **5.** a surprise   **6.** the thunder   **7.** fog   **8.** companion   **9.** a struggle   **10.** inch

E.   **1.** foam   **2.** vivid   **3.** harbor   **4.** ivory   **5.** trail   **6.** root   **7.** trunk

F.   **1.** over two million acres   **2.** rugged, with vividly colored mountains   **3.** flows of naturally hot water that come directly from the center of the earth   **4.** point out the trails and the dangers   **5.** walk alone into the mountains, set up a tent, and stay for a few days   **6.** in Wyoming

Unit 17

C.   **1.** F   **2.** T   **3.** T   **4.** T   **5.** F   **6.** T   **7.** T   **8.** F   **9.** T   **10.** T   **11.** F   **12.** T

D.   **1.** b   **2.** c   **3.** a   **4.** a   **5.** a   **6.** a   **7.** c   **8.** b   **9.** a   **10.** b

E.　**1.** hand-me-down　**2.** break up　**3.** obligation　**4.** make up　**5.** harmony

F.　**1.** make up　**2.** offend　**3.** siblings　**4.** offended　**5.** neglect　**6.** grateful
　　7. acquaintances　**8.** obligated

Unit 18

C.　**1.** T　**2.** T　**3.** F　**4.** T　**5.** F　**6.** F　**7.** T　**8.** T　**9.** F　**10.** F　**11.** T　**12.** T　**13.** F

D.　**1.** closed down　**2.** came about　**3.** do without　**4.** check out of　**5.** do...
　　over　**6.** closed up　**7.** checks up on　**8.** came down with　**9.** came along with

E.　**1.** feast　**2.** stage　**3.** idle　**4.** precede　**5.** rip　**6.** applause　**7.** architect

F.　**1.** concentrating　**2.** idly　**3.** assume　**4.** desire　**5.** entitled　**6.** do without
　　7. correspondence　**8.** lease

Unit 19

C.　**1.** F　**2.** F　**3.** T　**4.** T　**5.** F　**6.** T　**7.** F　**8.** T　**9.** T　**10.** F　**11.** T　**12.** F　**13.** F

D.　**1.** broke down　**2.** get on with　**3.** got in(to)　**4.** get by with/get by on
　　5. broken in　**6.** broke up　**7.** got away; broken into　**8.** got off

E.　**1.** get on　**2.** disaster　**3.** gasoline　**4.** get off　**5.** break in　**6.** awkward
　　7. velocity　**8.** gauge

F.　**1.** curve　**2.** brake/decelerate　**3.** decelerate/brake　**4.** collided
　　5. velocities/velocity　**6.** collision/impact　**7.** peak　**8.** gasoline

Unit 20

C.　**1.** T　**2.** F　**3.** F　**4.** F　**5.** F　**6.** F　**7.** F　**8.** T　**9.** T　**10.** T　**11.** T　**12.** F
　　13. F　**14.** T　**15.** T

D.　**1.** dimension　**2.** elements　**3.** at money　**4.** the immigrant　**5.** at her
　　voice　**6.** chemical properties　**7.** the angle　**8.** the calorie　**9.** the
　　disaster　**10.** damage　**11.** the music

E.　**1.** grip　**2.** roar　**3.** rival　**4.** program　**5.** tie　**6.** intensity

F.　**1.** basketball　**2.** the Boston Celtics and the Los Angeles Lakers　**3.** the
　　Celtics　**4.** tied　**5.** the Celtics　**6.** their programs　**7.** the clock

Unit 21

C.　**1.** F　**2.** T　**3.** T　**4.** T　**5.** T　**6.** T　**7.** F　**8.** T　**9.** T　**10.** T　**11.** T　**12.** F
　　13. T　**14.** T　**15.** T

D.　**1.** the smoke　**2.** a match　**3.** the dignity　**4.** the arson　**5.** symmetry
　　6. velocity　**7.** peninsula　**8.** ratio　**9.** the wall

E.　**1.** ash(es)　**2.** arsonist　**3.** block　**4.** bright　**5.** sweep out　**6.** moralize
　　7. chimney　**8.** broom　**9.** set

F.　**1.** flames　**2.** brightened　**3.** ashes　**4.** incendiary　**5.** arson　**6.** spotted
　　7. matches　**8.** extinguishers　**9.** stand by　**10.** put out/extinguished

Unit 22

C. 1. F 2. T 3. F 4. T 5. T 6. F 7. F 8. F 9. T 10. T 11. F 12. T 13. F 14. F 15. F

D. 1. institute 2. kindness 3. insistence 4. exclusion 5. corruption 6. arrangement 7. corruption 8. alienate

E. 1. count on 2. go on with 3. giving out 4. come out with 5. gone back on 6. back down 7. (a) looks up to (b) bring off 8. (a) live down (b) count...out

F. 1. territory 2. arranged 3. went back on 4. menace 5. propaganda 6. sneaky 7. alienated 8. justice 9. count on 10. dilemma

Unit 23

C. 1. F 2. T 3. T 4. F 5. F 6. T 7. T 8. F 9. F 10. T 11. T 12. F 13. T

D. 1. insane 2. vision 3. female 4. come to 5. scar 6. exhaustion 7. sex

E. 1. pass on 2. break out 3. get on with 4. come to 5. got over 6. breaks up 7. passed out 8. came out with 9. broken in 10. get by with

F. 1. break out 2. fatal 3. got over 4. handicapped 5. female 6. cope 7. prescribe 8. relief

Unit 24

C. 1. F 2. T 3. T 4. F 5. T 6. T 7. T 8. F 9. T 10. T 11. T 12. F 13. F 14. T

D. 1. format 2. revise 3. bring out 4. invalid 5. leave out 6. heading 7. ambiguous

E. 1. a 2. c 3. a 4. d/j 5. b 6. g/h 7. f 8. e 9. m 10. k 11. d/j 12. l 13. p 14. o 15. n 16. r

F. 1. looking up 2. comprehend 3. reference 4. interrupt 5. relevant/pertinent 6. irrelevant 7. format 8. heading 9. left out 10. refer

Unit 25

C. 1. F 2. F 3. T 4. T 5. T 6. T 7. F 8. T 9. F 10. T 11. T 12. F

D. 1. detective 2. verdict 3. charge 4. execution 5. admit 6. hold up/theft 7. prohibit 8. motivation 9. testimony

E. 1. d/g 2. c/f 3. b 4. e 5. a 6. h

F. 1. hold up 2. pistols 3. hand over 4. cleared out 5. panicked 6. detectives 7. juvenile 8. testify 9. charged 10. testimony 11. conviction

Words Assumed for Volume 1

a	baby	brother	correct	east
able	bad	brown	cost	easy
about	ball	build (built)	could	eat
absent	bank	busy	country	egg
after	bath	but	cousin	eight
again	be (am, is,	buy (bought)	cow	elephant
age	are, was,	by	cry	eleven
ago	were, been)		cup	end
air	beautiful		cut	enough
all	because	call		enter
almost	become	can		etc. (etcetera)
already	bed	can't	dance	every
also	before	car	dark	explain
always	begin	cat	daughter	eye
an	beside	centimeter	day	February
and	best	chair	dead	Friday
animal	better	chicken	December	face
another	between	child	desk	fall (n)
answer	big	(children)	different	false
any	bird	church	difficult	family
anybody	black	city	dinner	famous
anyone	blackboard	class	dirty	far
anything	blood	clean	do	fast
anywhere	blue	clock	doctor	fat
apple	board	clothes	dog	father
April	boat	clothing	dollar	feel
are	bone	coat	door	feet
arm	book	coffee	dormitory	female
arms	born	cold	down	few
arrive	both	color	dream	fifth
as	box	come	drink	find
ask	boy	complete	drive	fine
at	bread	continue	during	finger
August	breakfast	cook	each	finish
aunt	bring	corner	ear	fire

first	high	laugh	mouth	our
fish	him	learn	move	ours
five	himself	left	movies	ourselves
flag	his	leg	much	out
floor	hit	lesson	music	over
flower	hold	letter	must	
fly	holiday	library	my	
food	home	life	myself	page
foot (feet)	hope	like		paper
forget	horse	listen		parent
forth	hospital	little	name	part
forty	hot	live	near	party
four	hotel	long	necessary	past
free	hour	look	need	pay
friend	house	a lot of	neighbor	peace
from	how	love	never	pen
front	hundred	lunch	new	pencil
fruit	husband		news	permit
future			newspaper	person
		Miss	next	(people)
	I	Mr.	nice	picture
garden	ice	Mrs.	night	plane
get	idea	machine	nine	play
gift	if	magazine	no	please
girl	important	mail	nobody	police
give	in	make (made)	noise	poor
go	inside	male	none	practice
gold	interest	man (men)	no one	pretty
good	into	many	(no-one)	price
good-bye	is	map	north	problem
gram	it	marry	nose	put
grandfather	its itself	may	not	
grandmother		maybe	nothing	
grass	job	me	now	queen
green		mean (v)	nowhere	question
		meat	number	quiet
	key	medicine		
hair	kilogram	meet		
half	kilometer	meter	ocean	radio
hand	king	might	o'clock	railroad
handsome	kiss	milk	of	rain
happy	kitchen	million	off	read
hat	knife	minute	office	red
have	know	mistake	often	remember
have to		money	old	repeat
he		month	on	return
head	lady	moon	once	rice
hear	land	more	one	rich
help	language	morning	only	right
her	large	most	open	river
herself	last (adj)	mother	or	road
here	late	mountain	other	room

round	somehow	tea	two	why
run	someone	teach	type	wife
	something	telephone		will
	sometimes	tell		winter
sad	somewhere	ten	umbrella	with
salt	son	test	uncle	woman (women)
same	song	thank	understand	word
say	soon	the	university	work
school	sorry	their	up	would
second	soup	them	us	write
see	south	themselves	use	wrong
sell	speak	then		
send	spell	therefore		
seven	spend	these	very	year
she	spoon	they		yellow
ship	sport	thin		yes
shirt	spring	thing	wait	yesterday
shoe	stand	think	wake	you
shop	start	third	walk	young
short	stone	this	wall	your
should	stop	those	want	yourself
show	story	thousand	warm	yourselves
shut	street	three	wash	
sick	strong	throw	watch	
side	student	time	water	
sing	study	today	way	
sister	subject	tomorrow	we	
sit	such	tonight	weather	
six	sugar	too	week	
sleep	summer	tooth	well	
slow	sun	top	west	
small	swim	train	what	
smile		tree	when	
snow		true	where	
so	table	try	which	
soap	take	twelve	white	
some	talk	twenty	who	
somebody	tall	twice	whom	

In addition, the following closed sets have been assumed:

days of the week
months of the year
cardinal numbers
ordinal numbers

APPENDIX
C

Words in Volume 1

Numbers refer to **volume** and unit.

accept, **1**-1
address, **1**-6
advantage, **1**-12
afternoon, **1**-15
air force, **1**-18
airplane, **1**-2
airport, **1**-2
allow, **1**-8
ambition, **1**-14
ambulance, **1**-16
apartment, **1**-3
apply, **1**-1
army, **1**-18
around, **1**-19
artist, **1**-14
assign(ment), **1**-8
attempt, **1**-1
audience, **1**-9
automobile, **1**-2

back, **1**-16
bacon, **1**-15
band, **1**-25
barn, **1**-19
baseball, **1**-10
basement, **1**-12
beach, **1**-9
beef, **1**-15
bell, **1**-8
bench, **1**-9
bicycle, **1**-11
bill, **1**-24

bleed/blood, **1**-16
blow, **1**-4
body, **1**-16
boot, **1**-17
boring, **1**-9
boss, **1**-5
bowl, **1**-15
break, **1**-16
brick, **1**-12
bridge, **1**-11
bus, **1**-2
business, **1**-5

cafeteria, **1**-8
camera, **1**-7
camp, **1**-21
campus, **1**-8
card, **1**-21
careful/less, **1**-5
carry, **1**-7
cave, **1**-21
cent, **1**-6
chair, **1**-12
change, **1**-17
chapter, **1**-8
cheap, **1**-6
cheese, **1**-15
choose, **1**-8
clear, **1**-4
clerk, **1**-6
climb, **1**-21
coast, **1**-23

collect (call), **1**-24
college, **1**-1
comedy, **1**-25
comfortable, **1**-12
commit, **1**-22
common, **1**-16
communicate, **1**-6
company, **1**-5
compete, **1**-10
complete, **1**-1
concert, **1**-9
contract, **1**-14
cool, **1**-21
corn, **1**-19
cost, **1**-21
course, **1**-8
crime, **1**-22
cross, **1**-11
crowd, **1**-10

date, **1**-21
decide, **1**-3
declare, **1**-20
deep/depth, **1**-23
deliver, **1**-6
dial, **1**-24
direction, **1**-21
dissappear, **1**-22
distance (long), **1**-24
dormitory, **1**-1
dress, **1**-17
dry, **1**-4

dull, **1**-25

early, **1**-4
earth, **1**-23
edge, **1**-11
electricity, **1**-3
elementary school, **1**-1
else, **1**-25
embassy/ambassador, **1**-20
emergency, **1**-24
employ(ee), **1**-5
empty, **1**-2
enemy, **1**-18
enjoy, **1**-7
entertainment, **1**-9
envelope, **1**-6
ever, **1**-21
examine, **1**-16
excited, **1**-7
excuse, **1**-16
expensive, **1**-6
experience, **1**-14

factory, **1**-5
fan, **1**-10
fan, **1**-23
farm, **1**-19
fear, **1**-22
fence, **1**-19
fever, **1**-16
field, **1**-19
fight, **1**-18
film, **1**-25
finally, **1**-13
fog, **1**-23
forbid, **1**-20
force, **1**-20
forecast, **1**-4
foreign, **1**-6
fork, **1**-15
fortunately, **1**-14
frequent, **1**-24
fresh, **1**-15
frighten, **1**-18
fun, **1**-25
funny, **1**-9
furniture, **1**-3

game, **1**-10

garage, **1**-12
gas, **1**-12
geography, **1**-23
glad, **1**-7
glass, **1**-15
gloves, **1**-17
golf, **1**-9
government, **1**-20
grade, **1**-8
graduate, **1**-1
ground, **1**-23
group, **1**-10
grow, **1**-19
guard, **1**-18
guess, **1**-13
guest, **1**-12
gun, **1**-18

handle, **1**-20
hang up, **1**-24
hard, **1**-23
hate, **1**-22
head, **1**-20
health, **1**-16
heat, **1**-12
heavy, **1**-13
helicopter, **1**-18
high school, **1**-1
hill, **1**-23
hobby, **1**-9
honest/honor, **1**-20
horn, **1**-11
horrible, **1**-18
hurry, **1**-11
hurt, **1**-16

ill, **1**-16
impersonal, **1**-24
indoors, **1**-10
insect, **1**-21
instrument, **1**-24
insure, **1**-13
intersection, **1**-11
interview, **1**-5
invitation, **1**-13
item, **1**-13

jacket, **1**-17
jail, **1**-22

joke, **1**-25
juice, **1**-15
jungle, **1**-23

kill, **1**-18

landlord/lady, **1**-3
lane, **1**-11
last (v), **1**-7
lawn, **1**-12
lawyer, **1**-14
lease, **1**-12
leather, **1**-17
leave, **1**-7
license, **1**-14
light, **1**-13
light, **1**-3
limit, **1**-13
lobby, **1**-21
local, **1**-24
lose/loss, **1**-10
low, **1**-14
luggage, **1**-7

maid, **1**-14
message, **1**-24
middle, **1**-11
midnight, **1**-22
military, **1**-18
mirror, **1**-17
motel, **1**-7
move, **1**-11
mud, **1**-23
murder, **1**-22
mystery, **1**-22

navy, **1**-18
neighborhood, **1**-3
noon, **1**-8
nurse, **1**-14

odd, **1**-25
operator, **1**-24
opinion, **1**-20
orchestra, **1**-9
ounce, **1**-13
outdoors, **1**-10

Words in Volume 2

Numbers refer to **volume** and unit.

above, **2**-8
abroad, **2**-22
absent, **2**-1
accident, **2**-10
according to, **2**-11
account, **2**-12
act(or), **2**-23
adapt, **2**-22
add, **2**-12
advanced, **2**-1
advertisement, **2**-17
afraid, **2**-18
age, **2**-5
agriculture, **2**-13
alone, **2**-5
among, **2**-5
amusement, **2**-23
ancient, **2**-22
anniversary, **2**-5
annual, **2**-2
appropriate, **2**-9
approximately, **2**-22
area, **2**-3
arrangements, **2**-22
arrest, **2**-7
article, **2**-17
astronomy, **2**-24
at least, **2**-22
attack, **2**-7
aunt, **2**-5
author, **2**-17
available, **2**-3
avenue, **2**-25

avoid, **2**-7

bag, **2**-4
bake, **2**-4
ballet, **2**-23
bargain, **2**-9
basic, **2**-19
basketball, **2**-14
beat, **2**-7
believe, **2**-17
belt, **2**-9
biology, **2**-19
blanket, **2**-6
blind, **2**-6
block, **2**-3
boil, **2**-4
bomb, **2**-8
borrow, **2**-12
breathe, **2**-6
bring, **2**-12
busy, **2**-5

cabin, **2**-25
cake, **2**-4
calendar, **2**-22
cancel, **2**-23
capital, **2**-11
carry, **2**-4
cash, **2**-12
cattle, **2**-13
cause, **2**-16

center, **2**-10
Centigrade, **2**-15
century, **2**-13
certain, **2**-14
chalk, **2**-1
charge, **2**-9
chemical, **2**-16
chemistry, **2**-19
circle, **2**-23
climax, **2**-23
closet, **2**-25
cloth, **2**-9
coin, **2**-12
collect, **2**-24
command, **2**-8
comment, **2**-11
complain, **2**-25
complex, **2**-24
compulsory, **2**-1
condition, **2**-6
constitution, **2**-11
construct, **2**-25
contest, **2**-14
control, **2**-8
convenient, **2**-3
cooperation, **2**-20
cotton, **2**-9
count, **2**-12
couple, **2**-5
court, **2**-7
cover, **2**-9
crop, **2**-13
cry, **2**-5

Words in Volume 3

Numbers refer to **volume** and unit.

jealous, **3**-14
join, **3**-20
journey, **3**-3

keep, **3**-15
kind (adj), **3**-23
kiss, **3**-14
knee, **3**-19
knock, **3**-16

labor, **3**-2
laboratory, **3**-23
lake, **3**-11
lay, **3**-16
layer, **3**-6
lecture, **3**-1
let, **3**-14
liberty, **3**-18
lightning, **3**-11
line, **3**-23
literature, **3**-1
load, **3**-3
loose, **3**-4
loyal, **3**-20
luck, **3**-24

mad, **3**-21
magic, **3**-12
majority, **3**-18
manufacture, **3**-2
marine, **3**-10
mass, **3**-10
match, **3**-21
maximum, **3**-13
mental, **3**-12
metric, **3**-10
mile, **3**-5
million, **3**-5
mind (v), **3**-11
mind (n), **3**-23
minimum, **3**-13
minority, **3**-18
miracle, **3**-22
model, **3**-12
modest, **3**-21
motor, **3**-3

naked, **3**-4
nation, **3**-20

necessary, **3**-1
neck, **3**-19
negative, **3**-7
negotiate, **3**-2
neither, **3**-7
nightmare, **3**-12
normal, **3**-19
novel, **3**-1
numerous, **3**-12

object, **3**-6
occasion, **3**-25
occupation, **3**-2
offer, **3**-2
opposition, **3**-18
orange, **3**-11
ordinary, **3**-25
oriental, **3**-22
otherwise, **3**-25
ought to, **3**-14
owe, **3**-13
oxygen, **3**-21

party, **3**-18
pass, **3**-21
passenger, **3**-3
per, **3**-16
period, **3**-25
permanent, **3**-6
phrase, **3**-7
physical, **3**-12
plural, **3**-7
poem/poet, **3**-1
poison, **3**-9
pole, **3**-21
political, **3**-18
popular, **3**-4
population, **3**-18
porch, **3**-16
positive, **3**-7
poverty, **3**-18
powder, **3**-10
practical, **3**-4
praise, **3**-1
pray, **3**-22
precious, **3**-13
prison, **3**-9
procedure, **3**-8
process, **3**-6
professional, **3**-21
profit, **3**-25

prompt, **3**-5
protect, **3**-9
provide, **3**-17
psychology, **3**-10
punctual, **3**-25
pupil, **3**-23

questionnaire, **3**-10
quite, **3**-25

rapid, **3**-5
rate, **3**-13
ready, **3**-24
real, **3**-6
realize, **3**-21
rear, **3**-16
reason, **3**-3
recently, **3**-19
recognize, **3**-7
regularly, **3**-5
religion, **3**-22
reluctant, **3**-11
rely (on), **3**-14
remove, **3**-4
repay, **3**-13
represent, **3**-18
request, **3**-25
research, **3**-10
resign, **3**-24
reveal, **3**-7
review, **3**-1
rise, **3**-8
risk, **3**-20
roar, **3**-21
rocket, **3**-10
route, **3**-5
ruin, **3**-16
rule, **3**-1
rush, **3**-8

safe, **3**-9
sample, **3**-25
scarce, **3**-20
scholarship, **3**-23
scream, **3**-9
second, **3**-5
seem, **3**-19
select, **3**-20
seminar, **3**-1
separate, **3**-6

Words in Volume 4

Numbers refer to **volume** and unit.

Index

Words in Volume 5

Numbers refer to **volume** and unit.